Se

Maximize Your Life B… You Do.

SEEK FIRST

There is more to this book!

Make sure to visit **SeekFirstBrand.com** to become part of our community and stay connected with our inspiring video series! Scan the QR code below for access!:

SCAN ME

Connect with the author at DanielZiedins.com

The Mission of Seek First:

SEEK FIRST

Seek First exists to awaken a generation to pursue God first in every area of life. We are a Kingdom movement committed to helping people build their lives, families, businesses, and ministries on eternal foundations—aligned with God's priorities, not the world's patterns.

As part of Thy Kingdom Network, we are uniting ministries, churches, and individuals through bold collaboration and unwavering obedience to Jesus. At the heart of this movement are the Seek First Warriors—men and women who live courageously for Christ in every sphere of influence: business, sports, arts, education, and everyday life. They reflect Heaven's values, shift culture, and maximize every area of their lives for God's glory.

Our Mission Is To:

- Equip believers with practical tools to live out Matthew 6:33 in real life.
- Disciple through action—in thought, health, spirit, business, relationships, and everyday habits.
- Inspire culture change by raising up leaders who reflect Jesus in how they think, live, work, love, and lead.
- Advance the Gospel by building up Kingdom-minded communities and movements empowered by the Holy Spirit.

The 7 Pillars of a Seek First Life:

We believe every area of life is an opportunity for Kingdom impact. That's why our framework is built on 7 biblical pillars that help believers live fully surrendered and purpose-driven lives:

- **Mind** – Renew your thoughts and align with truth. (Romans 12:2)
- **Body** – Honor God by stewarding your health. (1 Corinthians 6:19-20)
- **Spirit** – Pursue deep, daily intimacy with God. (1 Corinthians 6:17)
- **Business & Finances** – Build and manage with eternal purpose. (Matthew 6:21)
- **Lifestyle** – Let your daily habits reflect Kingdom values. (1 Corinthians 10:31)
- **Relationships** – Love sacrificially, forgive freely, and cultivate unity. (John 13:34)
- **Kingdom Building** – Live on mission and obey the Holy Spirit boldly. (Matthew 28:19)

We're building a global Kingdom force. Through mentorship, resources, community, and challenges like the Seek First Warrior Challenge, we're raising up leaders who reflect Heaven and leave a legacy that matters. When you Seek First the Kingdom—in your thoughts, habits, and every decision—your life becomes a vessel for revival, transformation, and eternal impact. This is more than a mission. It's a movement. You were born for this. So rise up, Seek First, and let your life echo Heaven.

Dedication

To my beautiful wife, Katie, and our precious daughter, Ava—this book is for you both. Your love and support have been the driving force behind everything I do. My heart is to impact the world for Jesus, and I am so blessed to walk this journey together with you. May we continue to seek Him first in all things and make an eternal difference in the lives of those we touch.

With all my love,
Daniel

Follow our Family journey at: KD-Ziedins.com

Table of Contents:

Introduction

"The LORD bless you and keep you; The LORD make His face shine upon you, And be gracious to you; The LORD lift up His countenance upon you, And give you peace." – Numbers 6:24-26

I don't believe you're holding this book by accident. My prayer is that it won't just be words on a page but a turning point in your life. This book is more than information—it's an invitation. An invitation to step into a life where seeking God first isn't just a concept, but a reality that transforms every area: your relationships, health, finances, and purpose. If you take these truths to heart, I believe you'll look back and see this as the moment everything changed.

Jesus gave us a powerful key to life in *Matthew 6:33: "Seek first the Kingdom of God and His righteousness, and all these things will be added to you."* That's not just a suggestion—it's a promise. When we align our lives with God's priorities, everything else falls into place. That's what this book is about: helping you build a life that reflects Heaven, walking in the fullness of God's plan, and finishing strong with a legacy that impacts eternity.

When you seek first the Kingdom, you stop chasing the world—because everything you need starts chasing you.

To help you get the most out of this book, I've included practical steps, faith declarations, action steps, and a prayer section at the end of each chapter. I encourage you to really take your time with each one—reflect on them, speak the declarations out loud with faith, and pray the prayers with an open heart. Don't just read—apply. Because knowledge isn't power—applied knowledge is. I truly believe that if you engage with this book fully, you'll walk away changed.

But before we go any further, let me share a little of my story.

My Journey of Seeking First

My family is from Latvia, a small nation that once lived under the grip of Soviet rule. When the Soviet Union collapsed, the country was thrown into turmoil. In the midst of the chaos, a rare opportunity for my family to escape appeared—but we had to move quickly. My family left with nothing but the clothes on their backs—literally. No luggage was allowed, so my parents layered on as many clothes as they could on our family, sweating through a scorching day to escape into the unknown. When they finally made it to Toronto, Canada, of all places, we had nothing. No home. No money. That's when I was born, my family slept on newspapers and from there worked tirelessly to build a new life from the ground up. At just 12 years old, I started working in construction as a General Contractor. It might sound crazy, but those early years really shaped me. I learned what it meant to take responsibility, to work hard, and most importantly, to trust God in every season. Years later, I began hitting the streets of Hamilton every week with the girl of my dreams—who would later become my wife. We weren't part of a big organization. We just had a passion to love people where they were at, to bring hope to the hopeless, and to point people to Jesus. That's when Love on Hamilton was born. What started as a few people saying "yes" to God has now grown into Love on The World, a global ministry on a mission to reach the lost, ignite believers, and help people experience the same radical love and provision that transformed our lives. And the beautiful, full-circle part of it all? The very things my family lacked when they came to

Canada—shelter, support, hope, purpose—are the very things we now provide for others through our ministry. What once was our greatest need has now become our greatest assignment. Only God can write a story like that. I often stand in awe at how far He's brought us, and I'm overwhelmed with gratitude. From my family sleeping on newspapers to launching global outreach, this journey is living proof that when you Seek First the Kingdom of God, He truly does take care of the rest. So wherever you're starting from, know this: God has a plan for your life (Jeremiah 29:11). He is not just your provider—He is your source. And if you'll trust Him with everything, He will take what the world calls broken and build something beautiful for His glory. Through it all, I've seen firsthand that God can take any situation—no matter how impossible—and use it for His glory. That's the heart of this book. He's calling you to step into something greater. And I believe this journey of seeking Him first will unlock doors you never imagined possible. When you live by Kingdom principles, lack becomes a thing of the past.

A Kingdom Invitation

This book is a personal journey, yes—but it's also a movement. A call to action. A Kingdom invitation.

The Seek First life isn't just about getting your priorities in order—it's about **becoming someone God can trust with influence**, someone He can use to bring light into dark places, hope into hopeless hearts, and truth into a world drowning in confusion.

As you read these pages, I want you to remember something:

Your obedience has impact far beyond what you can see.

This is about you—and the lives that will be changed *through* you.

The people you'll reach. The stories you'll carry. The legacy you'll leave.

You are part of something bigger than yourself. The Seek First life is the beginning of a chain reaction that can change families, cities, and nations—one surrendered step at a time.

What You'll Discover in This Book

- A clear framework for aligning your Mind, Body, Spirit, Business, Lifestyle, Relationships, and Kingdom Purpose with God's priorities—what I call the 7 Pillars of the Seek First Life.
- Practical strategies to maximize your time on Earth for God's glory.
- A roadmap to finish your race strong—so you don't just live well, but leave a **Kingdom legacy** that echoes into eternity.

Why Seeking First Matters

Time is your most valuable asset. You can't earn more of it, and once it's spent, it's gone forever. That's why how you choose to invest your time matters more than anything else. Every moment you spend pursuing God's Kingdom has eternal significance (Psalm 90:12). You're not just managing minutes—you're sowing seeds into eternity. As Rick Warren writes in The Purpose Driven Life, "Living for God's glory is the greatest achievement we can accomplish with our lives." And yet, we often get pulled in a thousand directions—hustling, striving, reacting. This book is your reminder to realign your focus, and your invitation to live with purpose, clarity, and impact. That's why I've made this book as practical and actionable as possible. I deeply respect your time. My goal isn't to give you another feel-good message or lofty idea. My goal is to equip you with Kingdom truths and daily strategies you can actually live out—starting today. Because seeking God first isn't just a good idea—it's the best decision you will ever make. When you prioritize His presence, His ways, and His Kingdom, everything else begins to fall into place. Peace replaces pressure. Purpose replaces confusion. Provision replaces lack. This isn't just a book to read—it's a guide to live by. A framework to realign your life with what matters most.

The greatest investment you'll ever make is seeking God first—because His return isn't just better... it's eternal.

SEEK FIRST

Action Steps to Get the Most Out of This Journey

This isn't just a book—it's a call to build your life on a Kingdom foundation. But transformation doesn't happen by accident. It comes through intentional, Spirit-led steps. Here's how to make the most of this journey:

1. Carve Out Daily Seek Time

Set aside at least 15 minutes a day—morning or evening—to pray, reflect, and journal what God is revealing to you through each chapter. These aren't just pages to read; they're invitations to encounter God. Don't rush it. Make space.

2. Walk It Out With Others

Growth multiplies in community. Grab a friend, your spouse, or a small group to go through this with you. Discuss it weekly. Pray for each other. Keep each other accountable. Want to connect with others on the same path? Join our online community at SeekFirstBrand.com.

3. Make Your Faith Public

Boldness is contagious. Post a photo of the book or share what God is teaching you as you go. Use the hashtag **#SeekFirstChallenge** and tag **@SeekFirstBrand**. Your testimony might be the spark that ignites someone else's fire.

4. Create a Kingdom Tracker

Grab a notebook and dedicate it to your journey through this book. Write down insights, prayers, steps of obedience, and the breakthroughs that happen along the way. It'll become a record of God's faithfulness—and fuel for your future seasons.

5. Ask God, "What's My Next Yes?"

This book will stir vision. Don't shelf it—*act on it.* As God speaks to you about an area of life to realign or a bold step to take, ask Him, *"What's my next yes?"* Then follow through, one faithful step at a time.

Remember—this isn't about perfection. It's about pursuit.
One step at a time. One "yes" at a time. That's how you build the Seek First life.

You're not reading this by accident—this is a divine appointment. You are one act of obedience away from unlocking something greater than you ever imagined. This is your moment. This is your time. God has incredible plans for your life. Let's step into them—together.

Now, let's begin.

Reference: The 7 Pillars of a Seek First Life

Rooted in Matthew 6:33, these pillars represent key areas of life to surrender to God, aligning every part of your life with His Kingdom purpose.

1. Mind: "Do not conform to the pattern of this world, but be transformed by the renewing of your mind." – Romans 12:2 Renew your thoughts daily and align them with God's truth.

2. Body: "Your body is a temple of the Holy Spirit... therefore honor God with your bodies." – 1 Corinthians 6:19-20 Steward your health for strength, clarity, and obedience.

3. Spirit: "But whoever is united with the Lord is one with Him in spirit." – 1 Corinthians 6:17 Cultivate daily intimacy and communion with God.

4. Business & Finances: "For where your treasure is, there your heart will be also." – Matthew 6:21 Work and manage money with Kingdom purpose and radical trust in God.

5. Lifestyle: "Whatever you do, do it all for the glory of God." – 1 Corinthians 10:31 Live with intentionality—your everyday choices matter.

6. Relationships: "Love one another. As I have loved you, so you must love one another." – John 13:34 Build meaningful connections rooted in love, forgiveness, and unity.

7. Kingdom Building: "Go and make disciples of all nations..." – Matthew 28:19 Advance the Gospel and live on mission, using your gifts and life for eternal impact.

Chapter 1: Life Upside Down

Some moments mark us forever—moments when God flips our perspective and changes everything we thought we knew about success, purpose, and what truly matters. This is one of those moments. It's the story that led me to start SeekFirstBrand.com. But more than that, it's the story that redefined my entire pursuit of life. It was January 2017, a pivotal season for me. I was stepping into entrepreneurship, chasing the dream of financial freedom, scaling businesses, and building what the world calls "success." From the outside, I seemed to be on the right track—hitting milestones, and doing what most would consider "winning." But inside? My heart was out of alignment. I was so focused on achieving that I was missing what mattered most. At the time, my now-wife and I—who were just dating then—frequently visited a dear friend in the hospital. Their situation was devastating—facing a failing body, fading dreams, and the slow unravelling of the life they once knew. Each visit was sometimes heavy as we prayed to contend for healing, but one particular night shook me to my core. We sat at this person's bedside praying, my heart aching as I watched them struggle. I prayed desperately, asking God why someone so full of faith and purpose had to endure such suffering. I pleaded for answers, for understanding. And then, in the stillness of that moment, as Katie was praying for our friend, God spoke to me and asked me to look at our friend and he said:

"This person is the most successful person you know."

I froze. It didn't make sense. How could that be true?

By every worldly standard, my friend had lost everything—their health, their career, their stability. But as I sat there, trying to process what God had just said, something inside me shifted. I began to see through His eyes. The Lord reminded me of 1 Samuel 16:7: *"People look at the outward appearance, but the LORD looks at the heart."* My friend, despite their suffering, had an unshakable faith. Their heart was steadfast, full of peace, completely anchored in God. Even in the face of death, they radiated a trust that defied logic. And in that moment, I realized—success in the Kingdom of God is entirely upside down. It isn't measured by money, achievements, or status. True success is about the condition of your heart, the depth of your faith, and your obedience to Him.

For weeks, I had been consuming content from "successful" entrepreneurs, chasing the lifestyle they flaunted. Yet, sitting in that hospital room, I saw a success that no amount of money could ever buy. And I knew I had been running in the wrong direction.

That night, a new mission was born in my heart—Seek First.

Matthew 6:33 became my foundation: *"Seek first the Kingdom of God and His righteousness, and all these things will be added to you."*

This wasn't about abandoning dreams or ambitions—it was about putting them in their rightful place. God first. Always. Everything else? Secondary. My friend's faith never wavered, even as they took their final breath. Their life—and their passing—left a permanent mark on me. They showed me what true success looks like: a life fully surrendered to God. I encourage you to live in such a way that your faith outlives you. True wealth isn't measured in dollars, but in a heart fully surrendered to God. This is why Seek First Brand exists. Our logo—a flipped Kingdom—is a reminder that the world's definition of success is completely inverted from God's. While the world chases wealth, fame, and power, God calls us to seek Him first. When we do, everything we truly need will follow.

Obedience to God's call is the only path to a life that truly counts.

This isn't just a brand. It's a calling.
It's a reminder for anyone who has ever felt torn between striving for success and surrendering to God's will. Let this be your wake-up call, as it was for me. Put Him first. Seek His Kingdom above all else. Everything that truly matters flows from there.

The Hidden Power of Humble Service

'A Revelation That Changed Everything'

There's a revelation God gave me a while back, and it's been stuck in my spirit ever since. It changed how I view life, success, ministry—everything. And honestly, I think if more believers caught this, it would flip the Church upside down (in the best way). It's one of those truths that feels so obvious once you see it—but so different from what the world teaches us to chase.

You know how, in the world's eyes, success often looks like having people serve you? If someone has a personal chef, a cleaner, a driver, a full-time assistant, most of us would look at that and say, "Wow—they're clearly doing well." or "They're crushing it" And to be honest, there's nothing wrong with having help. That's not the point. But the revelation God gave me was this: in His Kingdom, the sign of true success isn't how many people serve *you*... it's how many people you serve. It's not status—it's surrender. And the more hidden, humble, and lowly the act of service is, usually the more valuable it is in Heaven.

Even Jesus Himself—the Son of God, King of kings—said *"I did not come to be served, but to serve."* (Matthew 20:28) That alone should shift our entire approach to greatness.

Over the years, I've actually come across stories—real, powerful testimonies—of people who died, encountered Heaven, and came back. And one of the things they all seemed to say stuck with me deeply: In Heaven, humble service is seen as royalty. What we overlook here on Earth is often celebrated in eternity. The people we might never notice—those opening doors, wiping tables, stacking chairs—are honored like kings and queens in the Kingdom of God.

Recently, God brought all of that back to the front of my mind in the most unexpected moment. Katie and I went to pick up some hot dogs that had been donated by a church for the Jesus Festival. While we were there, their food bank happened to be open in the church. I noticed a line of people outside, waiting to come in. And standing at the door was a man… just quietly opening and closing the door for each person. That's it. He wasn't preaching. He wasn't leading. He wasn't being recognized. He was just there, faithfully managing the line so the space inside wouldn't get too packed.

And man… as I watched him, I got hit with this sudden wave of emotion. I don't even cry easily, but something hit me deep. It wasn't just a sentimental moment—it was spiritual. I felt the presence of God so strongly, like He was highlighting that man to me and saying, *"Look at him. That's what greatness looks like in My Kingdom."*

God showed me—so clearly—how pleased He was with this man. No one else probably noticed him. Most people likely walked right past. But in Heaven, I believe that moment was lighting things up. He was doing something so simple, so ordinary—but doing it with joy, humility, and love. And in that moment, I realized again how upside down the Kingdom really is.

If people could truly see how God sees service… I believe they'd be running to serve. I really mean that. If we had eyes to see how much it matters, how much God values those hidden, humble acts—we'd be *fighting* over who gets to stay late and clean up after church. People would be lining up to scrub the toilets, pour the coffee, and vacuum the sanctuary. Because when you understand how Heaven views service, no task feels too small. In fact, the smaller it is, the greater the honor.

It's not about being seen by people—it's about being seen by God.

That's the revelation I hope sinks into your heart. Because once you really grasp it—once it gets from your head to your spirit—you'll never see service the same way again. You won't be waiting to be asked. You'll start looking for any opportunity to serve, no matter how unglamorous it seems. You'll live with a new kind of passion—because you'll understand that greatness isn't found in being above people, but in lifting others up.

This is how Heaven sees success. This is the heart of Jesus. And I pray that as you read this, something awakens inside of you. That you start seeing through Heaven's lens. That your heart begins to beat for the hidden places where no one is clapping, but God is smiling.

Because in the Kingdom… the towel is greater than the title. And every simple act of service—when done with love—echoes into eternity.

Speak Life: Daily Declarations

"The tongue has the power of life and death, and those who love it will eat its

fruit." — *Proverbs 18:21*

Your words carry spiritual authority. When you speak life, align your heart with truth, and declare God's promises boldly, things begin to shift—inside and around you. Speak these declarations out loud every single day with faith and boldness. Watch how your life begins to align with what you speak.

7 Declarations to Flip the Script

- I choose to seek God's Kingdom first in every area of my life—above all else.
- I believe true success is found in surrender, not status. My heart, not my hustle, is what God values most.
- I trust that when I put God first, everything I need will be added to me in His perfect timing.
- I release the pressure to perform and receive the peace that comes from obedience.
- I reject the world's definition of success and embrace God's calling on my life.
- I am not defined by my achievements, but by my faith, love, and obedience to Christ.
- I commit to living a life fully surrendered to God's will, with my heart anchored in His purpose.

Let these words become the framework of your mindset. Speak them. Believe them. Live them.

Prayer

Father, thank You for showing me what true success looks like in

Your Kingdom. I repent for the times I've chased after worldly achievements, approval, and identity outside of You. Realign my heart today. Help me to seek You first in everything I do—not just in moments of need, but in every thought, plan, and desire. Strip away any pride, fear, or distraction that keeps me from full surrender. Teach me to value what You value. Give me the strength to walk by faith, to obey even when it costs me, and to trust that Your way is always better. Let my life be a reflection of Your priorities—not the world's. May I be known in Heaven not by what I build, but by how deeply I love, believe, and obey You. Let true success be found in Your presence alone. In Jesus' name, Amen.

Call to Action: Flip the Script

You've just explored what it means to live a Kingdom-centered life—where true success is measured by surrender, not status. Now it's time to respond with action. Don't just read about the Seek First life—step into it.

Step 1: Evaluate Your Pursuit

Set aside ten minutes today for quiet reflection. Ask yourself:

- Where am I still chasing worldly success instead of God's will?
- What area of my life is driven by self over surrender?

Write down one area where you can begin to shift your focus back to God's Kingdom.

Step 2: Flip One Thing

Choose one tangible way to live differently.

It could be saying no to an opportunity that distracts you from your calling, restructuring your morning around prayer instead of emails, or prioritizing family time over extra hustle.

Flip the old pattern—and watch God show up.

Step 3: Speak a Different Story

The world needs to hear what God's doing in you. Share a quick story online about how you're choosing to flip the script and live the Seek First life. Use **#SeekFirstChallenge** and tag **@SeekFirstBrand** to encourage others.

Step 4: Start Your Seek First Journal

On the first page, write this prayer:

"God, turn my life upside down if that's what it takes for me to seek You first. I surrender the way I thought it should go—lead me into something better."

Kingdom living starts with Kingdom thinking.

If you want to see a different result, you have to live by a different blueprint. The good news? Jesus already gave it to us.

Let's flip the script—and build on something eternal.

Chapter 2: What Does It Mean to Seek First?

What does it truly mean to seek first the Kingdom of God?
It's more than a concept—it's a complete reorientation of your life. It means God isn't an afterthought, a safety net, or just a part of your weekly routine. He becomes the foundation, the focal point, and the driving force behind everything you do.
Seeking first the Kingdom means surrendering your own plans, desires, and even relationships to His will, trusting that His way is infinitely better. It's about living under His rule and reign—where His priorities become your priorities, His mission becomes your mission, and His righteousness becomes the standard for how you live. It's more than a concept—it's a complete reorientation of your life. God isn't an afterthought, a safety net, or something you squeeze into your weekly routine.
He becomes everything.
The foundation.
The focus.
The reason behind everything you do.
Seeking first the Kingdom isn't about adding God to your life—it's about building your life on Him.

Seeking First Means Surrender

Seeking first the Kingdom isn't just about adding God into your plans—it's about surrendering the plan entirely. It's letting go of control and trusting that God knows better than we do. That sounds simple, but when it comes to your job, your money, your security—it's one of the hardest things you'll ever do.

Right before COVID hit in 2019, I was working full-time as a site supervisor in construction. The job was solid. I had a good salary, a work truck, benefits—the kind of setup people pray for. On paper, things looked great. I had stability. I had a plan. But during prayer one day, I felt God speak clearly: *"Quit your job."*

It didn't make sense. Not even a little. No backup plan. No savings cushion. No clarity on what was next. Just that one step: resign.

Everything in me wanted to reason with God: *"Now? What about my bills? My family? What if I'm just making this up?"* But deep down, I knew it was Him. I could feel it. And the longer I waited, the more unsettled I felt. So I obeyed.

I handed in my resignation and walked away from everything that had made me feel "safe." It was scary. But just a few weeks later, I connected with someone on Instagram who ended up mentoring me in e-commerce. That connection turned into a business. The business grew. And before I knew it, we had scaled it to over 35 people working for us and I got to work full-time from home for quite some time.

Looking back, I realize something crucial: **God was already preparing the path—I just had to walk in it.** But I never would've seen what He had in store if I wasn't willing to surrender what I was holding.

That season taught me that surrender isn't just about letting go—it's about trading up. When you hand over your plans, God gives you His. And His plans are always better.

Surrender isn't blind. It's not reckless. It's faith in action. It's saying, *"God, I don't need all the answers. I just need You."* When you seek first the Kingdom, you're not just adjusting your priorities—you're submitting to a whole new blueprint. God's mission becomes your mission. His timing becomes your rhythm. His dreams start to shape your decisions.

And it always starts with one moment. One step of obedience. One quiet 'yes.'

Let me say this: if you're feeling that tug in your heart—if God is asking you to lay something down, shift directions, or walk into the unknown—don't ignore it. The discomfort might be real, but the blessing on the other side is far greater than the security you're trying to hold onto.

God doesn't call us to play it safe. He calls us to follow. And when you choose surrender, you step into a life you couldn't build on your own—a Kingdom life marked by purpose, peace, and provision.

So what is He asking you to surrender? Whatever it is, lay it down. His hands are better than yours.

Understanding the Kingdom and His Righteousness:

What is the Kingdom of God?

Jesus tells us, *"The Kingdom of God is within you"* (Luke 17:21). The Kingdom isn't some far-off place—it's a present reality that transforms every part of your life when you submit to God's authority. His Kingdom is marked by love, justice, mercy, and truth. It's not about building our own platforms but expanding His reign in our hearts, our families, and the world around us.

What is His Righteousness?

Righteousness isn't something you achieve—it's something you receive through faith in Jesus Christ. Romans 3:22 says, *"This righteousness is given through faith in Jesus Christ to all who believe."* It's about living in right standing with God, walking in obedience, holiness, and trust. It's not just about following rules—it's about relationship.

Some Practical Steps to Seek First

Start Your Day with God

"In the morning, Lord, you hear my voice; in the morning I lay my requests before you and wait expectantly." – Psalm 5:3
Before you check your phone or get caught up in the chaos of the day, spend time with God in prayer and Scripture. Let Him set the tone for your day. I like to turn off all my notifications on my phone for fewer distractions throughout the day too.

Align Your Decisions with His Will

"Trust in the Lord with all your heart and lean not on your own understanding; in all your ways acknowledge Him, and He will make your paths straight." – Proverbs 3:5-6
Before making decisions—big or small—pause and ask, *"Lord, what do You want?"* Seek His direction rather than relying on your own understanding. The safest place to be is in the center of God's will—even when it doesn't make sense (Because sometimes it won't).

Surrender Your Plans to God

"You do not even know what will happen tomorrow... Instead, you ought to say, 'If it is the Lord's will, we will live and do this or that.'" – James 4:14-15

Your life is not your own. Surrender your ambitions and dreams to God, trusting that His timing and plans are always greater than yours. Surrender isn't weakness; it's choosing divine strength over human control.

Evaluate Your Priorities

Jesus said, *"Where your treasure is, there your heart will be also."* – Matthew 6:21

Write down your top five daily activities. Ask yourself: *Are these Kingdom-focused?* If not, make adjustments to prioritize what truly matters. When God is your first priority, everything else finds its rightful place.

Create a Life Mission Statement

"Commit your work to the Lord, and your plans will be established." – Proverbs 16:3

Define what it means to live for God's glory. Write down a personal mission statement that aligns your life with His Kingdom purposes. Take time to do this (even now), as this will help guide you for the rest of your life here on earth.

Fast and Pray

"Is not this the kind of fasting I have chosen: to loose the chains of injustice… to set the oppressed free?" – Isaiah 58:6

Set aside a day to fast from distractions—food, social media, entertainment. Use that time to realign your heart with God's purposes. Fasting doesn't just empty you of distractions; it fills you with God's presence. It also happens to be great for your health too!

Biblical Example

In Luke 10:38-42, we see two sisters, Mary and Martha. Martha was busy, distracted by tasks, while Mary simply sat at Jesus' feet, listening to Him. Jesus said Mary had *"chosen the good portion."*
This story is a powerful reminder: Seeking first the Kingdom isn't about doing more—it's about choosing Him first.

Speak Life: Daily Declarations

"The tongue has the power of life and death, and those who love it will eat its fruit." — *Proverbs 18:21*

There is power when you speak truth over your life. As you begin to live a Seek First life, let your words reflect your surrender, your faith, and your alignment with God's Kingdom. Speak these declarations out loud every single day with boldness and watch your perspective—and your path—begin to shift.

7 Declarations to Seek First

- I seek first the Kingdom of God and trust Him to provide everything I need.
- I align my decisions, goals, and priorities with the will of God, not my own.
- I choose to live with a Kingdom mindset, focused on eternity, not temporary gain.
- I surrender my plans, dreams, and timelines to God, trusting His perfect timing.
- I fix my eyes on Jesus, not on the distractions or opinions

of this world.

- I walk in righteousness by faith, fully accepted and empowered through Christ.
- I step out in obedience, even when it's uncomfortable, because I know every act of surrender draws me closer to the life God has for me.

Let these truths take root in your heart—and speak them until they overflow into action.

Prayer

Father, thank You for calling me to seek first Your Kingdom and Your righteousness. I confess the areas where I've put other things before You—my plans, my comfort, my ambition. I lay them down at Your feet. Teach me what it means to live fully surrendered. Align my priorities with Yours. Help me walk in obedience, not by what I feel or see, but by faith in Your Word. Strengthen my resolve to seek You daily—to rise in the morning with purpose, to make decisions with eternity in mind, and to trust Your way even when it costs me. Let my life reflect Your glory. Let my story point others to You. I seek first Your Kingdom—today and every day. In Jesus' name, Amen.

Call to Action: Realign the Foundation

Seeking God first isn't about adding Him to your schedule—it's about building your life *on* Him. It's about shifting from "God, bless my plans" to "God, lead my steps." This chapter lays the foundation—now it's time to activate it.

Step 1: Redraw Your Blueprint

Take a fresh sheet of paper or journal page and write down the 5 biggest areas of your life right now (examples: work, health, family, finances, faith, etc.). Next to each one, write how that area might look if it were truly aligned with seeking God first. Be honest. Then pray over it and ask the Holy Spirit, *"Which one do You want me to start with?"*

Step 2: Set Your Seek First Anchor

Pick a time and place to seek God daily. Keep it simple but consistent. Whether it's 15 minutes in the morning with your Bible and journal, or a walk with worship music after work—lock it in. **Treat it like a non-negotiable appointment with the King.**

Step 3: Create a "God First" Reminder

Choose a visual reminder to keep your focus aligned throughout the day. A sticky note with Matthew 6:33. A custom phone lock screen. A bracelet. A wallpaper. Let it prompt your heart back to the Kingdom every time you see it.

Step 4: Find Your Accountability

Text a close friend and say: *"I'm on a mission to seek God first in every area of my life. If you ever see me getting off track—remind me why I started."* Bonus: invite them to read the book with you and walk this out together.

Your life flows from what you seek first.
This isn't about adding pressure—it's about shifting perspective.
When God is truly first, *everything else starts falling into place.*
Now take that first step—and realign your foundation.

Chapter 3: Seek First in Your Mind Pillar #1

What if I told you that the greatest battles you'll ever face aren't fought with your hands—but with your thoughts? Your mind is the control center of your life. Every thought you entertain either leads you closer to God's truth or further into fear, doubt, and distraction. The reality is this: If the enemy can take hold of your mind, he can derail your destiny. But if you learn to align your thoughts with God's Kingdom, nothing can stop you from walking in His perfect will.

Every thought is a seed—what you plant will grow. Sow truth, reap peace.

That's why Jesus told us to seek first the Kingdom of God (Matthew 6:33). Seeking first begins in your mind—before your actions, before your words, before anything else. You cannot have a positive life and a negative mind.

My Mind Was the Real Battlefield

For a long time, I thought the biggest battles in life were the external ones—trying to figure out how to grow a business, lead a ministry, provide for my family, make decisions, solve problems. But I eventually realized that the hardest battles weren't out there… they were happening silently, right between my ears. There was a season in my life where, on the surface, everything looked like it was going great. Business was booming. Ministry was growing. I was busy—in a good way. From the outside looking in, it probably looked like I was thriving. But internally? My mind was not at peace. I'd lie in bed at night with a racing heart and a restless mind. No matter how much was going right around me, my thoughts were loud and relentless. *What if I blow this? What if I fail? What if I'm not enough? What if I let everyone down?* Even in the midst of so much blessing, the pressure felt overwhelming—and the lies felt real. One day, it all hit at once. The pressure to perform, provide, and keep everything together was getting to me. In a quiet moment, I heard that familiar lie creep in: "*You're not enough. You're going to let everyone down.*" It shook me. I could feel the fear starting to take hold. But right then, something rose up in me. I remembered: It is written. I grabbed my Bible, flipped to 2 Corinthians 10:5, and said it out loud: "I take every thought captive and make it obedient to Christ." That moment became a line in the sand for me. I realized I couldn't keep trying to hustle my way out of fear or overthink my way to peace. I had to fight back with something stronger than feelings—I had to fight with the Word. From that point on, whenever a lie came, I responded with Scripture.

"God has not given me a spirit of fear…"

"He will keep in perfect peace those whose minds are steadfast…"

"I can do all things through Christ…"

I didn't always feel like it in the moment, but I kept speaking truth. And slowly, the lies started to lose their grip. The fear didn't scream as loud. The anxiety didn't hold the same weight. Now, don't get me wrong—it wasn't a magic switch. This didn't go away overnight. It became a daily decision to align my mind with God's Word, over and over again. But with time, truth started to take over. My thinking began to shift. My peace returned. And even though the pressure didn't disappear, I learned how to walk through it with confidence and clarity. To this day, I still have to check my thoughts. When I feel pressure rising or I start drifting into worry, I stop and ask: "What voice am I listening to right now?" Because if it doesn't sound like God—it has no business taking up space in my head.

And I want to tell you the same thing: you CAN win the war in your mind. Not by trying harder, but by filling your mind with truth—truth that sets you free. The real battle isn't changing your circumstances—it's renewing your mind.

This fight is real. But so is your victory.

The War for Your Mind

Right now, there's a battle happening inside you. Every day, your thoughts are shaped by what you hear, what you see, and what you believe. The enemy's greatest weapon is deception; your greatest defence is truth. Romans 12:2 calls us to break free from the patterns of the world by renewing our minds with God's truth. Why? Because when we allow our minds to be shaped by fear, comparison, or negativity, we unknowingly align ourselves with the enemy's strategy.

But there's good news: You don't have to stay trapped in negative thinking. Jesus showed us how to fight back.

Jesus' Victory in the Wilderness

Picture this: Jesus, alone in the wilderness, fasting for forty days. Weak, hungry, and physically exhausted. That's when Satan strikes, whispering lies and offering temptations (Matthew 4:1-11).

But Jesus doesn't argue. He doesn't negotiate. He responds with one weapon—Scripture.

"It is written…" He declares God's truth with authority, and the enemy is defeated.

This moment wasn't just about Jesus overcoming temptation—it was a blueprint for us. The Word of God is our greatest weapon in the battlefield of the mind. When the enemy whispers, *"You're not good enough,"* you respond, *"It is written: I can do all things through Christ who strengthens me" (Philippians 4:13).*

When fear creeps in, you say, *"It is written: God has not given me a spirit of fear, but of power, love, and a sound mind" (2 Timothy 1:7).*

Victory starts when you take control of your thoughts.

How to Renew Your Mind Daily

Transformation doesn't happen by accident. Your life moves in the direction of your strongest thoughts—make sure they're Kingdom-centered. You have to be intentional about filling your mind with God's truth. Here's some ways you can do that:

Meditate on Scripture Every Day

Choose one verse each morning. Write it down. Speak it out loud. Let it sink into your heart. Philippians 4:8 tells us to fix our minds on what is *true, noble, right, pure, and praiseworthy.*

Keep a Gratitude Journal

Every night, write down three ways you saw God at work that day. Also, write 3 things you are grateful for each morning. This shifts your focus from problems to His faithfulness. *"Give thanks in all circumstances; for this is God's will for you"* (1 Thessalonians 5:18).

Memorize Key Scriptures

The Word of God is your ammunition. Start with these:

- **Romans 12:2** – *"Do not conform to the pattern of this world, but be transformed by the renewing of your mind."*
- **Isaiah 26:3** – *"You will keep in perfect peace those whose minds are steadfast, because they trust in You."*
- **2 Corinthians 10:5** – *"We take captive every thought to make it*

obedient to Christ."

When anxious thoughts come, speak these verses out loud. Watch how your mind completely shifts.

Turn Negative Thoughts into Prayers

Worried? Pray. Afraid? Pray. Frustrated? Pray. Instead of letting your thoughts spiral, give them to God. *"Do not be anxious about anything, but in every situation, by prayer and petition, with thanksgiving, present your requests to God"* (Philippians 4:6-7). 1 Thessalonians 5:17 reminds us to "pray without ceasing," emphasizing the importance of staying in constant communication with the Lord. Turn your thoughts into prayers throughout the day, keeping your heart aligned with His presence.

Replace Lies with God's Truth

Every time a negative thought comes, ask yourself: *Would God say this to me?* If the answer is no, replace it with Scripture. The enemy will tell you, *"You're not enough."* But God says, *"You are fearfully and wonderfully made" (Psalm 139:14).*

Your Mind, Your Choice

You have a choice every day: Let your thoughts be ruled by fear and negativity, or take control and align them with God's truth. Seeking first the Kingdom starts here. When your mind is filled with God's Word, your life will overflow with His power, peace, and purpose. Fill your mind with God's truth until there's no room for the enemy's lies.

Speak Life: Daily Declarations

"The tongue has the power of life and death, and those who love it will eat its fruit." — Proverbs 18:21

Your mind is the battlefield—and your words are your weapon. Every time you speak God's truth over your thoughts, you take ground. Don't stay silent in the war for your peace. Declare truth boldly, every day, and let God's Word reshape the way you think.

7 Declarations to Renew Your Mind

- My mind is renewed daily by the truth of God's Word, not the patterns of this world.
- I take every thought captive and make it obedient to Christ.
- God's peace guards my heart and mind in every situation—no matter what I face.
- I fix my thoughts on what is true, noble, right, pure, lovely, and praiseworthy.
- I have the mind of Christ—full of wisdom, clarity, and sound judgment.
- I do not entertain lies or fear. My thoughts are rooted in God's truth and purpose.
- Fear has no place in my mind, because perfect love casts out all fear.

Speak these out loud each day—especially when you feel the battle in your mind intensify. Your words shift your atmosphere.

Prayer

Lord, thank You for the power of Your Word that transforms and renews my mind. I surrender my thoughts to You today—every fear, every doubt, every lie that has tried to take root. Help me take every thought captive and make it obedient to You. Teach me to meditate on truth and resist the enemy's deception. Let Your peace reign in my mind and guard my heart from anxiety, confusion, and distraction. Fill me with clarity, focus, and faith. Let my thoughts be aligned with Heaven, and may they produce a life that reflects Your Kingdom. Today, I choose to seek You first in my thoughts—because where my mind goes, my life follows. In Jesus' name, Amen.

Call to Action: Win the War in Your Mind

Your thoughts shape your life. What you dwell on, you eventually live out. That's why renewing your mind isn't optional—it's essential. If you want to see transformation, it starts with what happens between your ears. Here's how to take authority over your thought life this week:

Step 1: Do a Thought Audit

Take a day to track the dominant thoughts that run through your mind. Set reminders on your phone every 3 hours and ask: What have I been thinking about? Is it true? Is it life-giving? Is it aligned with God's Word? Write down any recurring patterns you notice—especially lies, fears, or anxious loops.

Step 2: Replace the Lies with Truth

Take one negative thought you've been battling—maybe something like "I'm not good enough" or "It's all up to me." Now, find a specific Scripture that speaks the opposite. Write it out. Post it where you'll see it. Speak it out loud every time that lie tries to sneak in. You don't fight thoughts with thoughts—you fight them with the Word.

Step 3: Declutter Your Input

Choose one source of mental noise—social media, toxic conversations, constant news—and fast from it for 3 days. Replace that time with worship, the Word, or just silence. You'd be amazed at what God will speak when the volume of the world is turned down.

Step 4: Memorize a Mind-Anchor Verse

Pick one verse from this chapter (or one God highlights to you) and make it your "anchor verse" for the week. Meditate on it. Memorize it. Let it frame your thoughts when stress, fear, or distraction try to creep in.

Step 5: Share Your Testimony

Encouragement multiplies when it's shared. Post on social media or text a friend about how God is renewing your mind. Invite others to do the same using #SeekFirstChallenge.

Remember: when you renew your mind, you renew your direction. Let this be the start of a brand-new thought life.

You don't have to live captive to your thoughts—

You have the authority to take your thoughts captive and bring them under the Lordship of Jesus. This isn't just a mental shift. It's a spiritual breakthrough. Victory starts in the mind. Let the renewing begin.

Before You Turn the Page...

This journey doesn't stop here.

At the end of each 'pillar' chapter, you'll find a QR code that leads to a dedicated landing page focused on this specific pillar. These pages are frequently updated with new resources, teachings, videos, and tools to help you go even deeper—no matter when you got this book.

Make sure to bookmark the page and check back often for fresh updates and content designed to encourage and equip you.

You'll also gain access to our Seek First Community, where you can connect with other Kingdom-minded believers to discuss this pillar, share testimonies, ask questions, and grow together in faith.

Scan the QR code below and stay connected with what God is doing through this movement.

SEEK FIRST: MIND

Chapter 4: Seek First in Your Body Pillar #2

When we think about seeking first the Kingdom of God, we often picture prayer, worship, or serving others. But what if I told you that honoring God with your body is just as spiritual as lifting your hands in worship? The Bible makes it clear that our physical health is deeply connected to our spiritual walk. In 1 Corinthians 6:19-20, Paul reminds us that our bodies are temples of the Holy Spirit. That means how we treat our bodies is an act of worship. Good health is not vanity; it's stewardship. When you take care of your body, you are caring for the temple where God's Spirit dwells.

The Day I Realized My Body Was Holding Me Back

There was a season where I felt like I was running on fumes—mentally, spiritually, and physically. I was still showing up. I was still leading, still praying, still serving. But behind the scenes, I was dragging. My energy was low, my focus was off, and by mid-afternoon, I felt like I was already done for the day. I kept chalking it up to being "just tired" or "in a tough season." I'd tell myself I was fine because I was still being used by God. But deep down, I knew something wasn't right. I wasn't operating at full capacity, and the cracks were starting to show—not just physically, but spiritually too.

Then one day, everything clicked. I was out doing street ministry downtown, praying for people, handing out food, sharing the Gospel—things I love to do. This older man walked up to me. You could see the pain in his eyes. He was clearly going through it. As I started talking to him, I realized something sobering—I wasn't fully present. My mind was foggy. My body was aching. I was standing there, trying to encourage him, but I was distracted by how tired I felt. And it wasn't spiritual warfare. It wasn't burnout from ministry. It was from neglect—neglecting the very body God gave me to carry out the mission.

In that moment, I heard God speak so clearly: *"You're asking Me to use you, but you're not stewarding the vessel I've given you."* That hit hard. I'd never really considered how much my physical health impacted my spiritual availability. I'd been treating my body like an afterthought—skipping meals, grabbing junk food throughout the day, barely drinking water, ignoring the gym, cutting corners on sleep. And somehow I expected to run hard for God without collapsing. I was asking for Kingdom assignments while ignoring the condition of the vessel He'd asked me to steward.

That day, I made a decision: no more excuses. I didn't start with a massive fitness plan or try to go full-on overnight. I just started with what I had—cleaning up my meals, going to bed earlier, drinking water, moving my body daily, even if it was just some pushups in the garage or a walk after dinner. I started thinking like someone on mission. Because I am. We all are.

And almost immediately, things began to shift. I felt alive again. Focused in prayer. Present in conversations. I wasn't trying to power through the day—I had stamina. I had mental clarity. I had joy. And it wasn't about being shredded or trying to impress anyone. It was about being available. Useful. Sharp. Ready for whatever God had next.

That one shift—realizing that my physical health was part of my spiritual obedience—changed everything. And I want to encourage you with this: this isn't about fitness goals or trying to hit some unrealistic standard. It's about being ready. It's about honoring the temple God has given you so you can carry out the mission He's called you to. It's about having fuel in the tank when someone needs you. About having clarity when you need to hear God's voice. About showing up fully—not just spiritually, but physically too.

You don't need six-pack abs. You need strength. Focus. Endurance. You need your body to serve your calling—not to be the reason you have to slow down. Scripture says your body is a temple of the Holy Spirit (1 Corinthians 6:19). It's not something to be worshiped—but it is something to be *stewarded.* You can't run a race with a flat tire, and you can't fulfill your calling long-term if your health is falling apart.

So if you're feeling sluggish, foggy, or drained, don't just pray for more energy—ask yourself if you're stewarding what God already gave you. Your calling depends on your ability to show up. Start where you are. Take small steps. Build momentum. Because your obedience—even in the small things—will begin to unlock greater capacity for everything God has called you to do.

Your Body as a Temple

Imagine walking into a breathtaking cathedral, its architecture flawless, its atmosphere filled with peace. Now imagine that same cathedral neglected—dusty, broken, its beauty hidden behind years of disregard. The truth is, God designed your body as a sacred temple, meant to house His Spirit. When we neglect it—through poor nutrition, lack of rest, or a sedentary lifestyle—we hinder our ability to serve God with energy and focus.

Neglecting your health isn't just a physical issue; it's a spiritual one.

A tired, broken body limits a powerful calling.

Our bodies are not just for us; they are vessels through which God works in the world. When we take care of them, we honor Him and position ourselves to serve with strength and joy. As 1 Corinthians 10:31 declares, *"So whether you eat or drink or whatever you do, do it all for the glory of God."* Taking care of your health isn't just a good idea—it's an act of obedience and stewardship.

Here's Some Practical Steps to Steward Your Health

Master Your Daily Rhythms

Your body thrives on consistency. Going to bed and waking up at the same time each day regulates your natural rhythms and boosts your energy. Starting your day with intention—whether through prayer, stretching, or a nutritious breakfast—sets the tone for a productive and focused life. *"In the morning, Lord, You hear my voice; in the morning I lay my requests before You and wait expectantly"* (Psalm 5:3).

Fuel Your Body with Purpose

Food isn't just about taste—it's fuel for your mission. Every meal is an opportunity to nourish your body and mind. Prioritize whole foods, lean proteins, fruits, and vegetables. Avoid overindulgence, remembering Proverbs 25:16: *"If you find honey, eat just enough—too much of it, and you will vomit."* Eat in a way that energizes you to fulfill God's purpose, rather than weighing you down.

Strengthen Your Body to Serve

God designed your body to move. Regular exercise doesn't just keep you fit; it sharpens your mind, boosts your mood, and equips you for the demands of your calling. Whether it's walking, running, lifting weights, or even stretching, find a routine that challenges you. *"For physical training is of some value, but godliness has value for all things, holding promise for both the present life and the life to come"* (1 Timothy 4:8). Strengthen your body so you can serve God with endurance and passion.

Hydrate Like It Matters (Because It Does)

Your body is about 60% water, yet so many of us neglect hydration. Drinking enough water isn't just a health tip—it's a way to sustain the temple God has given you. Dehydration affects mental clarity, mood, and even your ability to focus in prayer. Treat hydration as a daily act of stewardship. *"Do you not know that your bodies are temples of the Holy Spirit?"* (1 Corinthians 6:19-20).

Sabbath: The Rest That Recharges You

Rest is not just a luxury, but a vital part of God's design for our lives. In Exodus 20:8-10, we are invited to set aside one day each week for Sabbath. This time of rest is important because God knows that constant striving can wear us down. Embracing rest allows our bodies and souls to be rejuvenated, so we can serve with renewed strength. It's an opportunity to prioritize sleep, unplug from the noise, and find stillness where God can speak to our hearts.

Build a Culture of Accountability

Stewarding your health isn't just about personal discipline—it's about community. Find an accountability partner who shares your desire to honor God with their health. Whether it's meal planning, exercising together, or simply checking in, accountability fosters consistency and motivation. *"As iron sharpens iron, so one person sharpens another"* (Proverbs 27:17).

Speak Life: Declarations

"The tongue has the power of life and death, and those who love it will eat its fruit." — Proverbs 18:21

The way you speak about your health shapes the way you live. Your body is a gift from God—a vessel to carry His presence, serve His purpose, and reflect His glory. Speak life over your body daily, and let your words build a stronger, Kingdom-driven you.

7 Declarations to Steward Your Health

- My body is a temple of the Holy Spirit, and I honor God in how I care for it.
- I am strong, energized, and equipped to fulfill the call of God on my life.
- I make disciplined choices in how I eat, rest, move, and recover.
- I reject laziness, neglect, and overindulgence—they have no place in my temple.
- God's grace empowers me to walk in health and wholeness, one step at a time.
- I steward my strength as a tool for worship, service, and impact.
- My health is not about perfection—it's about obedience, purpose, and alignment with God's plan.

Speak these every morning. Don't just aim for fitness—aim for faithfulness with your body.

Prayer

Lord, thank You for the incredible gift of my body—Your temple, created for Your glory. Forgive me for the times I've neglected or mistreated this vessel. Teach me to steward my health with intention, not vanity. Help me honor You in how I eat, rest, move, and live. Fill me with strength when I feel weak, discipline when I feel lazy, and clarity when I feel confused. Let my body reflect the truth of who You are—not just in appearance, but in purpose, energy, and resilience. Use my health to fuel the mission You've entrusted to me. May I live energized, focused, and ready to serve You well. I choose today to seek You first—even in how I care for my body. In Jesus' name, Amen.

Call to Action: Steward the Temple

When you take care of your body, you position yourself to serve God more effectively. Don't wait for a perfect plan. Take the first step today and invite God into your health journey.

Step 1: Start a Health Journal

Track your sleep, food, hydration, movement, and take inventory of how you feel physically. Are you tired, foggy, sluggish, or constantly drained? Ask yourself: *"Am I taking care of the body God has given me—or just trying to push through it?"* Write down 2-3 specific habits you know need to shift. Whether you use a digital app or a handwritten notebook, let this be your way of inviting God into your daily rhythm of health.

Step 2: Implement One New Habit

Choose one simple but impactful health habit to begin this week. It could be drinking more water, stretching each morning, cutting out processed sugar, going to bed earlier, or walking daily. Start small. Stay consistent.

Step 3: Find Accountability

Ask someone to join you on your journey. Encourage each other to be consistent in caring for your body as a form of worship. You weren't meant to do this alone.

Step 4: Prioritize Sabbath Rest

This week, intentionally set aside one day for full rest and restoration. Use the time to recharge physically, seek God spiritually, and reset emotionally. Rest is not laziness—it's obedience.

Step 5: Schedule Your "Temple Time"

Block out 30–45 minutes at least 3x this week to move your body. Treat it like an appointment with God—not to perform, but to steward. Pray before or during your workout. Invite the Holy Spirit into the process.

Step 6: Share the Journey

Post a photo or video showing how you're honoring your body today. Whether it's a healthy meal, workout, or Sabbath moment, use the hashtag #SeekFirstChallenge to inspire others to do the same.

Your body is a temple. Honor it. Fuel it. Move it. Rest it. And above all—surrender it to God. Your future requires a healthy, disciplined, Spirit-led you.

I hope you found a ton of value in Pillar #2: Seek First in Your Body.

Your health is not separate from your spiritual life—it's a key part of honoring God and walking in your purpose.

For more resources, tips, and encouragement on growing in your body for God's glory, scan the QR code below.
This page is frequently updated, so make sure to bookmark it and check back often.

And don't do this journey alone—join the Seek First community and connect with others who are pursuing health, strength, and purpose for the Kingdom.

Scan the code to get started.

SEEK FIRST: BODY

Chapter 5: Seek First In Your Spirit Pillar #3

Your spirit is the wellspring of your life—the place where your deepest connection with God resides. To seek God first in your spirit means to intentionally cultivate intimacy with Him through daily communion. It's the first and most important place from which all Kingdom living flows.

"But whoever is united with the Lord is one with Him in spirit." (1 Corinthians 6:17)

When your spirit is aligned with God, your whole life begins to reflect His heart. This is not about religion or ritual—it's about relationship. And like any relationship, intimacy requires time, intention, and communication.

Living Spirit First

There was a time when I got so caught up in doing things for God that I began neglecting time with God. I would wake up and immediately jump into my work or ministry plans. But over time, I noticed something missing. I was leading from emptiness. One morning, the Lord convicted me: "You're doing My work, but you're not sitting with Me.". I realized I had become more focused on producing than abiding. From that day forward, I committed to making time with God my top priority—before emails, phone calls, or even breakfast. And what I discovered was this: the more I abide in Him, the more fruitful I become (John 15:5). Seeking first in spirit changed my entire life. But there was a deeper revelation the Lord gave me during that same season—something I hadn't heard talked about much. I realized I wasn't just tired because I was too busy—I was spiritually depleted because I was living on yesterday's connection. I was trying to serve, lead, and pour out from moments I had with God days ago… weeks ago… and expecting it to carry me through today. That's when the Lord spoke clearly to my heart: "You're running on yesterday's connection." It hit me hard. I was functioning from spiritual memory instead of present intimacy. I knew then I couldn't afford to treat my spirit like a side note anymore. If I wanted to live a life that reflected God's Kingdom, I had to seek Him daily—freshly. Not as a task on my list, but as the foundation of my life. It wasn't about having another "quiet time." It was about protecting the secret place like my life depended on it—because it does. Your spirit is your root system. Just like a tree draws all its life and nourishment from what's underground, your strength, peace, and fruitfulness are drawn from the health of your spirit. If the root is dry, the fruit eventually withers. But when your spirit is filled, aligned, and in communion with God, every other part of your life begins to flourish. That's why it's so important to cultivate a spirit-first lifestyle—not out of obligation, but from a desire to walk in daily intimacy with God. Below are some practical ways to develop a deeper spirit-first rhythm in your life.

How to Cultivate a Spirit-First Life

Begin Every Day with God

Wake up and say, "Good morning, Holy Spirit." Start each day in prayer and the Word. Let Him speak before the world does.

Make Worship a Lifestyle

Worship doesn't need a stage or music team. Turn on worship in your home. Sing out in the car. Lift your heart to God at all times.

Listen for His Voice

Jesus said, "My sheep listen to My voice…" (John 10:27). Practice stillness and silence, and listen. He wants to speak more than we want to hear.

Cultivate Spiritual Disciplines

Prayer, journaling, Scripture memorization, worship, silence, solitude—these are spiritual practices that nourish the soul and build intimacy with the Father.

Speak Life: Daily Declarations

"The tongue has the power of life and death, and those who love it will eat its fruit." — Proverbs 18:21

Your spirit is where Heaven touches Earth. When you declare truth over your spirit, you awaken your inner life to God's presence, power, and purpose. Speak these out loud each day—*before the world gets a word in.* Let your words align your heart with the Kingdom.

7 Declarations to Awaken Your Spirit

- I am deeply connected to God and walk in daily intimacy with Him.
- My spirit is alive, aligned, and overflowing with the presence of the Holy Spirit.
- I hunger and thirst for righteousness, and I am filled with fresh fire from Heaven.
- I hear the voice of the Shepherd and follow His leading with confidence.

- My heart is fully surrendered to God's will, not my own.
- I abide in Christ and bear lasting fruit that glorifies the Father.
- My secret place is my strongest place—because it's where I'm filled, healed, and commissioned.

Speak these daily—and watch your inner life awaken to a whole new level of depth and clarity.

Prayer

Father, thank You for making my spirit one with Yours. I don't want to live disconnected or distracted. I want to live from the place of abiding. Awaken my heart to Your presence. Teach me to hear Your voice above the noise and to long for time with You more than anything else. Forgive me for every time I've replaced intimacy with activity. I don't want borrowed fire—I want fresh fire. Fan the flame in my spirit. Stir up hunger, stillness, and sensitivity. Let my secret place become a place of power, renewal, and revelation. I choose to seek You first in my spirit—today and every day. In Jesus' name, Amen.

Call to Action: Guard the Flame

When you live spirit-first, everything else flows from a place of life, peace, and presence. But intimacy with God doesn't happen by accident—it must be pursued and protected. Let today be the day you prioritize the health of your spirit.

Step 1: Build Your Secret Place

Choose a space in your home—a chair, a corner, a room—and dedicate it as your "altar." Make it a place where you meet with God daily. Set the tone with worship, Scripture, and stillness.

Challenge: For the next 7 mornings, go to your secret place before anything else—no phone, no distractions, just you and Him. Journal how it impacts your day.

Step 2: Fast from the Noise

This week, pick one major source of distraction and fast from it for 3 days. It might be social media, music, shows, podcasts—anything that's been louder than God's voice. Fill that space with prayer, worship, or Scripture instead.

Challenge: Journal what you sense during those quiet moments. Let your spirit relearn how to listen.

Step 3: Schedule a "Stillness Session"

Once this week, carve out 20–30 minutes to sit in silence. No music. No agenda. Just invite the Holy Spirit and be still. Let your spirit catch up with His presence. Journal anything He brings to your heart.

Step 4: Invite the Holy Spirit Into Your Routine

Every time you shift into a new part of your day (starting work, going to the gym, heading to bed), pause and simply pray: *"Holy Spirit, be with me in this moment."* You'll start to notice how present He really is.

Step 5: Share the Journey

Share a photo of your secret place or a takeaway from your quiet time and tag #SeekFirstChallenge. Your obedience might inspire someone else to cultivate their own spirit-first rhythm.

You weren't made to burn out—you were made to abide.
Your power flows from presence. Your clarity comes from communion. And your greatest weapon is a spirit fully alive in Him.

Fuel your spirit first—and watch everything else come to life.

Final Thoughts...

Your spirit is where Heaven meets Earth. When you put God first in your spirit, everything else aligns. Here are a few truths to carry with you:

"Intimacy with God is not a luxury—it's the lifeline of Kingdom living."

"Your greatest strength isn't in your schedule, your skill, or your strategy—it's in your secret place."

"Revival doesn't start in crowds—it starts in quiet communion."

"Before you build anything for God, make sure you're being built by God."

"You were created not just to do great things for God, but to walk closely with Him."

You know the drill—scan the QR code below to go deeper into this pillar.

SEEK FIRST: SPIRIT

And hey—don't keep this to yourself.

Share what God's teaching you through this book and tag us: @SeekFirstBrand.

Let's spread this movement of seeking Him first!

Chapter 6: Seek First in Your Business and Finances Pillar #4

"For where your treasure is, there your heart will be also." (Matthew 6:21)

Money and work are two of the biggest forces shaping our lives. They influence where we live, how we spend our time, and even how we view ourselves. Yet, for many people, faith and finances feel like separate worlds. But in God's Kingdom, nothing is separate. Your business, career, and bank account are not just practical necessities; they are tools God has given you to steward for His glory. Jesus wasn't against wealth. He was against wealth owning us. That's why He constantly challenged people to evaluate their hearts when it came to money. The question isn't whether you have money; it's whether money has you. If we truly believe that God is our provider, then everything we have belongs to Him. Our role is to steward His resources with wisdom, generosity, and a Kingdom-first mindset.

From Survival Mode to Kingdom Trust

Growing up in a family that started with nothing, money was always on my mind. Not in a greedy way—but in a survival way.
I was trained, without even realizing it, to think from a place of lack. *What if it runs out? What if there's not enough? What if I lose everything I worked for?* That kind of thinking followed me into adulthood. Even when I had plenty of work, the fear still lingered.
No matter how much I made, I couldn't shake the feeling that it could all disappear tomorrow. I'd read Scriptures about God being our provider. I believed it in theory. But deep down? I was still

trying to be my own provider.

Then one day, during prayer, God brought me to *Luke 12:24:*

"Consider the ravens: They do not sow or reap, they have no storeroom or barn; yet God feeds them. And how much more valuable you are than birds!"

That verse hit different. The ravens don't hustle. They don't store up in fear. They trust. And God provides. Every single day.

I realized then that my issue wasn't just financial—it was spiritual.

I didn't have a money problem. I had a mindset problem.

From that moment on, I began to pray differently.

Not, *"Lord, help me make more."*

But, *"Lord, help me trust more."*

I started giving more freely. I tithed with joy. I stopped hoarding. I stopped panicking. And every single time I needed provision—God showed up.

Sometimes it was through unexpected opportunities.

Sometimes it was through people I never expected.

But it always came. Every need met. Always on time.

Why This Matters...

The enemy wants you living in fear of not enough.

But God invites you into a Kingdom where He is more than enough. If you've been stuck in a poverty mindset—constantly worrying, stressing, striving—take a step back and ask:

"Who do I believe is my provider?"

Because if it's really God, then there's no need to fear.

Let that truth sink in:

You are worth more than the ravens.

And He's never let them go hungry.

The Kingdom Perspective on Business and Finances

You can't take your money with you when you die, but you *can* send it ahead. When we invest in what matters to God—spreading the

Gospel, helping those in need, building His Kingdom—our resources have eternal significance. If your business isn't building the Kingdom, then what is it building?
Jesus made this clear in the Parable of the Talents (Matthew 25:14-30). Three servants were given different amounts of money to manage while their master was away. Two invested wisely and multiplied what they had, while the third buried his talent out of fear. The first two were rewarded; the last was rebuked. What's the lesson here? God expects us to maximize what we've been entrusted with. Playing it safe or hoarding out of fear is not faithfulness—it's wastefulness.
But stewardship isn't just about how we manage money; it's about the posture of our hearts. If there's anything in our lives we're unwilling to surrender to God—our business, our income, our financial security—then that thing has become our master.

Practical Steps to Seek First in Business and Finances

Tithe and Give Generously

God doesn't need our money, but giving shows where our trust lies. Tithing (giving 10% of your income to the church) is a biblical principle that acknowledges God as your provider (Malachi 3:10). Beyond that, cultivate a spirit of generosity—support missions, help the poor, and be open-handed with what you have (2 Corinthians 9:6-8). When you give, you declare that money doesn't control you—God does.

Budget with Purpose

Money flows where it's directed. If you don't tell your money where to go, it will disappear. A Kingdom-focused budget prioritizes giving, saving, and wise spending. Proverbs 21:20 says, "The wise store up choice food and olive oil, but fools gulp theirs down." Be intentional. Every dollar should serve a purpose.

Work with Eternal Impact

Your job is more than a paycheck—it's a platform for ministry. Whether you own a business, manage a team, or work a 9-to-5, ask yourself, *How does my work advance God's Kingdom?* Excellence in your work glorifies God (Colossians 3:23-24). Treat every client, coworker, or customer as someone you can bless.

Work Hard. Rest Easy.

The world shouts, "Grind non-stop." But God whispers, "Be still and know that I am God" (Psalm 46:10). Resting isn't weakness. It's worship. It's not just about recharging your body—it's about renewing your trust. When you pause, you're declaring: "God is my source, not my striving." You can work with all your heart and still live with a heart at rest—because your security isn't in your hustle, it's in Him.

Heart Check: What Owns You?

A simple way to test where your heart is: *If God asked you to give up your business, your wealth, or your financial security today, could you do it?* If the answer is no, it's time for a reset.
You can either trust in riches or trust in the One who provides them. Only one will never fail.

Steps to realign your heart:

- **Increase Your Value in God**: Spend more time in His Word and in prayer. The more you value Him, the less you cling to material things.

- **Surrender What's in the Way**: If something is competing with God for first place, be willing to let it go. This might not mean giving it up entirely, but it does mean loosening your grip.

Speak Life: Daily Declarations

"The tongue has the power of life and death, and those who love it will eat its fruit." — Proverbs 18:21

Money and work are powerful forces in our lives—and the way you speak about them matters. When your words align with Heaven, your business and finances shift from striving to stewardship. Speak these declarations daily to renew your mindset and align your work with Kingdom purpose.

7 Declarations to Align Your Work & Wealth

- I work as unto the Lord—not for man, applause, or status.
- My finances are a tool for Kingdom advancement and eternal impact.
- I trust God as my provider and steward every resource with wisdom and integrity.
- My heart is fully surrendered to God—no possession or paycheck comes before Him.
- I give generously, joyfully, and consistently, knowing it honors God and multiplies impact.
- I walk in financial peace, not fear, because I know who my Source is.
- My work is worship, and I build not for my name, but for the glory of His Kingdom.

Let these declarations reset your mindset every day—because how you see work and money shapes how you steward them.

Prayer

Lord, thank You for entrusting me with work, resources, and influence. You are my Source. Help me to work with excellence and integrity, always remembering that I serve You first. Teach me to manage my finances with wisdom, to give with joy, and to live with open hands. Expose anything in my life that I've put before You—any security I've placed in wealth instead of You. Help me surrender every area of my business and finances so that I can live fully aligned with Your purposes. May my work reflect Heaven. May my wealth serve Your mission. May my heart stay fixed on You. In Jesus' name, Amen.

Call to Action: Put Your Treasure Where Your Heart Is

Your business and finances were never meant to be separate from your faith—they're meant to fuel your Kingdom impact. Today, make a bold move to realign your work and money with God's priorities.

Step 1: Start or Strengthen Your Tithing

If you haven't already, begin tithing faithfully—10% of your income, given joyfully to your local church. If you already do, ask God how He may be calling you to grow in generosity.

Challenge: Give today—even something small. Let your obedience shift the atmosphere over your finances.

Step 2: Create a Kingdom Budget

Build (or review) a budget that reflects Kingdom values: giving, saving, and stewarding wisely. Track your spending to see where your heart is really invested.

Challenge: Categorize your last week of spending—how much of it reflects your calling, generosity, or Kingdom purpose?

Step 3: Reflect & Surrender

Ask the Lord: Is there anything I wouldn't give up if You asked? Be honest. Whether it's your business, income, title, or sense of control—give Him your full "yes."

Challenge: Write it down, pray over it, and surrender it with intentionality. Also, In one paragraph, describe how your business, job, or financial life could look if fully surrendered to God's mission. Be bold. Dream big. Write it like a declaration. Post it near your workspace and read it aloud daily this week.

Step 4: Bless Someone Financially

Ask God to highlight someone you can bless—an unexpected gift, paying for a meal, giving to a missionary or cause. The amount doesn't matter—the obedience does. Giving breaks greed and activates joy.

Step 5: Share What You're Building

Encourage others by sharing what you're realigning in your business or finances. Use the hashtag #SeekFirstChallenge to multiply the movement.

You're not just managing money—you're multiplying impact. Every dollar can be a seed. Every workday can be worship. When you seek first in your business and finances, you stop chasing provision and start walking with the Provider.

Money makes a terrible master—but it's a powerful servant.

When you submit your work and finances to God, you don't lose control—you gain purpose. He becomes your source, your strategy, and your CEO.

Work with Him. Build with Him. Give like you trust Him.

You're not just building a business—you're building the Kingdom.

Money is a tool. Work is a mission field. And when you align your heart, hustle, and habits with Heaven, everything shifts.

Remember: God doesn't need your money—He wants your trust.

So whether you're an entrepreneur, employee, or visionary in the making, keep your eyes on the eternal. Let your business reflect the heart of the King.

Want more wisdom, tools, and Kingdom business training?
You know the drill—scan the QR code, get equipped, and stay connected with our community of purpose-driven leaders.

I'll see ya on the Business Pillar page.
Let's build what lasts forever.

SEEK FIRST: BUSINESS

Chapter 7: Seek First in Your Lifestyle Pillar #5

Living a life that seeks God first isn't just about adding more spiritual "to-do's" to your week—it's about becoming someone who is fully surrendered. It's not just about what you do; it's about who you are becoming. When seeking God becomes your lifestyle, it touches everything—your schedule, your decisions, your conversations, even the quiet moments when no one is watching. It's the awareness that God doesn't want to be a guest in your life—He wants to be the foundation you build everything on.

For a long time, I thought I had the Christian life figured out. I grew up around church culture. I knew the rhythms: show up on Sunday, try to be a good person, serve where you can, repeat next week. And don't get me wrong—there was value in all of it. But deep down, something felt missing. It felt like I was doing the right things, but not walking in the fullness of what I read about in Scripture. It started to feel routine. Predictable. Like I was following Jesus *on paper*—but not in power.

Then one day, I opened the book of Acts with fresh eyes. And what I saw wrecked me—in the best way. Ordinary people were living with radical boldness. They weren't just attending services—they were being the Church. Filled with the Holy Spirit. Preaching the Gospel. Healing the sick. Casting out demons. Watching miracles unfold *daily*. It wasn't polished or perfect. It wasn't only happening on a platform. It was messy, raw, real… and alive. And in that moment, something clicked deep inside me:

There's more.

And not just more for pastors or missionaries—but more for every single believer. For *me*. For *you*. That realization changed everything. I started praying differently. Not, "God, help me get through my week," but "God, how do You want to use me today?" I started waking up with expectation. Believing that everywhere I went—whether it was the grocery store or a gas station—could become a place where Heaven touched Earth.

And I kid you not, the moment I stepped out with that kind of faith, everything changed. I began seeing things I'd only read about. People being healed right in the streets. Deliverance happening in our home. Tears flowing in parking lots as someone encountered the Gospel for the first time. Not because I had it all together or had some special anointing—but simply because I made myself available. God isn't looking for perfect people. He's looking for surrendered ones.

That's when it all shifted. I stopped seeing my faith as something I turned on for Sunday and off during the week. I stopped compartmentalizing my life—where "ministry" only happened at church or on a mission trip. I realized that when you truly seek God first, *everything becomes ministry*. Your job site becomes a mission field. Your errands become assignments. Your downtime becomes divine opportunity.

Now, I live with this phrase at the front of my mind: **Your ministry is wherever your feet are.** That simple truth changed the way I walk through life. The grocery store? It's ministry. The gym? Ministry. At the movies? Ministry. Even standing in line at the bank or at the playground with our daughter—I'm on assignment. You are never "off duty" in the Kingdom of God. The Holy Spirit doesn't clock in and out.

Every so often, especially when I'm in the middle of something ordinary, I'll literally stop and look down at my feet. And I'll remind myself: *"Wherever these feet are, that's where the Kingdom is."* Because if Jesus is living in you, then every step you take carries purpose. That's the lifestyle of seeking God first. Not just on Sundays. Not just when it's convenient. But in the in-between, the unnoticed, and the everyday.

And I want you to know—you don't have to wait for the perfect moment to start living like this. You don't need a stage, a title, or a ministry card. You already have what it takes: the Spirit of God inside of you and the call to bring the Kingdom wherever you go. So stop waiting. Start walking. Heaven is closer than you think.

"You don't need a platform to be powerful.
You just need to be present—fully surrendered, fully available.
Don't let busyness or routine rob you of divine moments.
You were made to live on mission.
Every place you step is an opportunity for God to move.
So keep your eyes open. Keep your heart ready.
And from time to time, just look down at your feet.
That's where the adventure begins."

The Heart of a Kingdom Lifestyle

Living with a Kingdom focus means understanding that every moment matters. It's not just about Sundays, ministry work, or mission trips—it's about how you live when no one is watching. It's how you speak to the barista at the coffee shop, how you handle frustration in traffic, how you treat your spouse and kids after a long day. You don't drift into a God-centered life; you choose it daily.

Our lives don't belong to us. They've been entrusted to us by God for a greater purpose. As Paul reminds us in 1 Corinthians 6:19-20: *"You are not your own; you were bought at a price. Therefore, honor God with your bodies."* The message of the Gospel is not simply, "God loves me, period." It's, "God loves me so that I might make Him known." Your life is your platform. The way you live is either drawing people closer to Christ or pushing them further away. *"Whatever you do, work heartily, as for the Lord and not for men." (Colossians 3:23)*

I want to share a powerful revelation God gave me years ago—one that deeply impacted my walk with Him and continues to shape how I live today:

The Ripple Effect:
How One Small Decision Can Change Everything!

Imagine this:

David is a husband, father of two, and a hardworking employee. One evening, he faces a simple choice—go to bed on time or stay up to binge-watch a show while snacking on chips. It seems trivial. But let's follow the impact of that one decision.

David stays up late, mindlessly eating. The sugar and processed food make his sleep restless. He wakes up groggy, hits snooze one too many times, and skips his morning prayer. Now he's late. In the rush, he snaps at his wife, rushes out the door without breakfast, and speeds through traffic in frustration.

At the drive-thru, his impatience boils over. His coffee order is wrong, which irritates him even more. By the time he gets to work, his mood is wrecked. His boss calls him out on his attitude, and instead of responding with humility, David lashes out: "I've given this company years! I don't deserve this." His boss, already at his limit, fires him on the spot.

David heads home, humiliated and angry. His wife, still upset from their morning fight, confronts him. The argument escalates into a heated exchange that shakes the foundation of their marriage. Meanwhile, their kids, who left the house unfed and unsettled, take their frustration to school, lashing out at classmates.

All of this—set in motion by one seemingly insignificant decision.

Recognizing the Starting Point

It wasn't his boss's attitude. It wasn't his wife's frustration. It wasn't the traffic.

It started with that small, careless choice. Staying up late, neglecting his health, and ignoring discipline set off a chain reaction.

The Bible warns us about this:

"Do not be deceived: God is not mocked, for whatever one sows, that will he also reap." (Galatians 6:7-8)

Every choice—no matter how small—is a seed. What you sow will grow into something, whether you realize it or not. The question is: Are you sowing into the Spirit or into the flesh?

Correcting the Momentum

Here's the good news: Momentum works both ways. Poor choices create a downward spiral, but good decisions can build a life of blessing. *Proverbs 24:16* reminds us: *"Though the righteous fall seven times, they rise again."* Mature believers recognize when they've gone off course and correct quickly. David could have changed the outcome at several points:

- He could have apologized to his wife before leaving.
- He could have taken a deep breath and chosen patience in traffic.
- He could have responded to his boss with humility instead

of pride.

Repentance is more than saying sorry. It's turning around, shifting your actions, and planting new seeds for a better future. Discipline today creates freedom tomorrow. The choices you make now will either chain you or change you.

Creating a Positive Ripple Effect

Every small decision matters. When you start your day with prayer and worship, when you respond with kindness instead of irritation, when you put God first in your decisions—it creates a ripple effect that transforms not just your life, but those around you. If you don't like what you're reaping, it's time to change what you're sowing. You must take your words seriously—every single one. Scripture is clear: "The tongue has the power of life and death, and those who love it will eat its fruit." (Proverbs 18:21) Your words carry weight. If you want to walk in greater authority, it starts with how you speak. Katie and I are practice this often.. We've made it a habit to gently call each other out when we hear one of us say something negative. For example, if I say, "My shoulder is killing me," she might ask, "Do you want me to come into agreement with that?" That always snaps me out of it—because we know the Bible says, "If two of you agree on earth about anything they ask, it will be done for them by My Father in heaven." (Matthew 18:19) Of course, I don't want agreement with pain or negativity. But this simple practice reminds us just how easily we can declare the wrong things without even realizing it. If you pay very close attention, you'll notice something interesting: people often live the very lives they declare. Ever notice how the person who always says, "I'm always late," usually is? Or the one who says, "I never have any luck with cars," constantly ends up with lemons? It's almost like their words are prophesying their reality! I sometimes joke that if you want to meet someone with a lot of faith, talk to someone with back pain. They'll describe their pain with such conviction and certainty, it's like they believe with all their heart that it will never go away. Sadly, many people start to identify with their pain or struggle, and they can't even imagine life without it.

But Jesus gives us a better way.

Let's remember what He said: "I tell you that everyone will have to give account on the day of judgment for every idle word they have spoken." (Matthew 12:36)

The good news? Just like negative words can create a ripple effect of destruction, words of life can create a ripple effect of breakthrough.

"Faith is the substance of things hoped for, the evidence of things not seen." (Hebrews 11:1)

So even when you feel pain, declare healing: "I am healed in Jesus' name." When you feel weak, say: "I am strong." When fear creeps in, speak: "God has not given me a spirit of fear, but of power, love, and a sound mind." (2 Timothy 1:7)

Speak life until your life begins to shift. Because it will. Your words can set the course of your future. **Start declaring truth, and you'll be amazed at the ripple effect Heaven releases in your life.**

The Challenge

We all have our "bag of chips" moments. The question is: How do we respond?

- **Recognize** when you're heading in the wrong direction.

- **Stop. Repent.** Turn back toward God's path.
- **Sow differently.** Choose discipline, prayer, and intentionality.

Your choices today determine the life you live tomorrow.

Some Practical Steps

- **Align Your Activities with Kingdom Goals** *(Ephesians 5:15-16)* - Are your hobbies, social media use, and daily habits reflecting God's purpose?
- **Practice Hospitality** *(Hebrews 13:2)* - Open your home to neighbors, church members, and those in need.
- **Be a Light in Your Workplace and Community** *(Matthew 5:16)* - Even in ordinary moments, let your actions point people to Jesus.

Speak Life: Daily Declarations

"The tongue has the power of life and death, and those who love it will eat its fruit." — Proverbs 18:21

Your lifestyle is not just what you do—it's who you are when no one is watching. When you speak God's truth over your daily actions and rhythms, your habits begin to reflect Heaven. Declare this over your life each morning and let your lifestyle preach the Gospel without a word.

7 Declarations to Align Your Lifestyle with the Kingdom

- I seek God first in every part of my daily life—from the small choices to the big ones.
- My habits reflect Heaven's values: love, integrity, generosity, and grace.
- I live with intentionality, knowing every moment is an opportunity to glorify God.
- I choose discipline over distraction and purpose over passivity.
- My lifestyle points others to Jesus—even in the ordinary routines of my day.
- I welcome the Holy Spirit into every area of my life—public and private.
- I am a living testimony of God's love, and my life echoes the values of His Kingdom.

Let your lifestyle declare what you believe before you ever speak a word.

Prayer

Heavenly Father, thank You for the gift of life and the everyday opportunities to reflect You. I don't want to compartmentalize my faith—I want it to influence how I think, how I live, how I speak, and how I love. Help me seek You first in the daily rhythms of my life, not just in spiritual moments, but in every interaction, every decision, and every habit. Align my lifestyle with Your Kingdom. Make me a light in dark places. May the way I live spark hunger for You in others. Teach me to live with boldness, gratitude, generosity, and grace—just like Jesus did. I surrender every moment, every task, every step to You. In Jesus' name, Amen.

Call to Action: Turn Habits Into Heaven's Rhythm

Your lifestyle preaches the loudest sermon you'll ever give. Every choice, every conversation, every unseen moment is shaping your legacy. Seeking first in your lifestyle means *living like God is Lord of all, not just some.*

Here's how to start realigning your daily life this week:

Step 1: Audit Your Daily Rhythms

Take one day to log your time—hour by hour. How much of your day is being invested in things that build your faith, strengthen relationships, or serve others? Are your habits feeding your soul—or just filling your schedule? Write down three small shifts that would make your days more Kingdom-focused.

Step 2: Practice Intentional Hospitality

Invite someone over this week or go out of your way to show kindness to a stranger. Jesus used meals, conversations, and shared spaces to demonstrate love. So can you.
Challenge: Create one moment this week to serve or welcome someone intentionally.

Step 3: Establish a "Kingdom First" Morning Routine

Start your day with God—before social media, before the to-do list, before the chaos. Even just 10 minutes in the Word, prayer, or stillness can realign your mindset. Set your alarm, make your coffee, and make time for what matters most.

Step 4: Turn One Routine Into Ministry

Pick something you already do—school drop-off, working out, grocery shopping—and ask, "How can I bring the Kingdom here?" Pray for someone. Share a kind word. Ask how you can serve. The more you train yourself to look for opportunities, the more God will open doors.

Step 5: Create a "Rule of Life"

Write out 5 personal lifestyle statements that reflect how you want to live. Example: I speak life. I prioritize rest. I live generously. I respond in love. I stay present with people. Post it somewhere visible and revisit it weekly.

Step 6: Share What's Shifting

Your transformation can spark someone else's. Post online or tell a friend what you're learning as you seek God first in your lifestyle. Use #SeekFirstChallenge to inspire others to examine how they're living.

God doesn't just want your Sunday—He wants your Tuesday morning, your lunch breaks, your bedtime routines, your errands, your leisure. When you align your lifestyle with His Kingdom, you become a living signpost pointing people to Jesus.

When God is first, everything becomes sacred.
Your meals. Your margin. Your routines. Your rest. Don't chase balance—live by rhythm. Let your daily life become a living testimony of a heart fully surrendered.

You don't have to change everything overnight—just start living on purpose today.

Your lifestyle is your loudest sermon.

It's not just what you say—it's how you show up, day in and day out. From the smallest habits to the biggest decisions, every moment is a chance to reflect Heaven. "The Kingdom isn't just built on platforms—it's built in parking lots, coffee shops, and conversations." Here's your reminder: God wants to use your ordinary to do the extraordinary. Don't wait for perfect conditions—just be available. **"Discipline today builds the destiny you'll walk in tomorrow."**

You know what to do—scan the QR code to dive deeper into this pillar and get fresh, ongoing resources to help you keep seeking Him first in your everyday life. "Your lifestyle is the echo of what you truly believe—let it shout Jesus."

SEEK FIRST: LIFESTYLE

This page is updated often, so bookmark it, revisit it, and stay connected.

And don't forget—share what you're learning and tag us @SeekFirstBrand. Let your journey inspire someone else.

"Every decision is a seed. Sow Kingdom. Reap legacy."

Keep living it.

Keep sowing it.

Every step you take is Kingdom territory.

Chapter 8: Seek First in Your Relationships Pillar #6

At the core of God's Kingdom lies one central theme: love. Relationships are not just part of our lives; they are the very fabric of our faith. Jesus made this abundantly clear in Matthew 25:40, saying, "Whatever you did for one of the least of these brothers and sisters of mine, you did for me." Our relationships with others are not just a side note to our Christian walk—they are its heartbeat. By embracing love, practicing forgiveness, and fostering meaningful connections, we mirror the heart of the Gospel in our daily lives. Love is the currency of the Kingdom. Invest it generously.

Unity Through Mission

One of the biggest lessons I've learned in marriage—especially being married to my amazing wife, Katie—is that unity doesn't come from getting everything right. It doesn't come from avoiding conflict, having perfect communication, or always seeing eye-to-eye. Real unity comes from shared pursuit. From chasing the same Person and the same purpose—together. Marriage, at its core, isn't about perfection. It's about direction. It's about waking up each day and choosing, not just to pursue each other, but to pursue Jesus side by side.

Something shifts when a husband and wife stop obsessing over who's right and start asking the better question: *What's the mission?* Because the moment you get on mission together, the little things lose their grip. In our marriage, Katie and I have found that the less we focus on trying to fix each other, and the more we focus on doing what God's called us to do, the closer we naturally become. It's like the distance closes when our eyes are fixed on the same point—Jesus. We're not pulling each other toward our own agendas—we're walking in the same direction, step by step, shoulder to shoulder.

That doesn't mean we don't have our moments. Of course we do. We've had disagreements, seasons of pressure, and misunderstandings just like anyone else. But over time, I've learned to stop and ask myself one simple question when the tension starts to rise: *"Will this matter a million years from now?"* That question has saved me more times than I can count. Because when I step back and view things through the lens of eternity, most of the things that try to steal our peace—don't even make the cut. They may feel big in the moment, but when you zoom out, you realize how small they really are.

It's in those moments of tension where we have to realign—realign with each other, yes, but more importantly, with God's purpose for our marriage. Our mission is to serve God, love each other well, and reflect His Kingdom here on Earth. And when we remember that, it brings clarity. It brings peace. It brings perspective. Because unity doesn't come from trying to control the other person—it comes from both people surrendering to the One who holds it all together.

The truth is, it's not always easy—but it is possible. When Jesus is your focus, you stop keeping score. You stop measuring your relationship by temporary standards. You stop fighting *against* each other and start fighting *for* each other. When both of you are committed to seeking God first, He becomes the glue that holds everything together. Not performance. Not flawless communication. Not perfectly planned date nights or agreement on every issue. Just Jesus.

That's where the strength comes from. That's where the joy lives. That's how love grows. Over time, I've learned that the greatest thing you can bring into your relationship isn't a solution—it's surrender. Surrender to God's way. Surrender to His timing. Surrender to His mission. Because when you're both surrendered, your marriage becomes unstoppable. It becomes a living picture of the Gospel—a story of grace, unity, and purpose in motion.

And here's something else I've discovered—something that often gets overlooked: sometimes, the very mission you've been called to is what will protect your marriage. When you're busy building together, you don't have as much time to tear each other apart. When you're loving people, reaching the lost, discipling others, and pushing forward for the Kingdom, your focus shifts from internal frustrations to eternal impact. You become teammates in the truest sense—not just sharing a house, but sharing Heaven's vision.

So if you're in a relationship or married and you're feeling stuck, disconnected, or constantly frustrated, try shifting the question. Instead of, "Why isn't this working?" ask, "What are we building together?" Because more often than not, the unity you're longing for isn't found in solving every issue—it's found in saying yes to the mission God placed in front of you.

Relationships as a Battlefield for the Kingdom

If the enemy can divide relationships, he can disrupt Kingdom momentum. That's why relationships—especially Kingdom ones—are not just emotional spaces, they're spiritual battlegrounds.

The health of your relationships will directly impact the strength of your calling. That includes your marriage, your friendships, your church family, and even how you relate to strangers.

Why? Because the enemy knows that *where there is unity, God commands a blessing* (Psalm 133:1–3). But where there is division, bitterness, or unresolved offense, it creates space for confusion, isolation, and spiritual stagnation.

That's why the Bible calls us to not let the sun go down while we are still angry (Ephesians 4:26)—because unresolved offense is one of the enemy's favorite entry points.

When we choose to love, forgive, and lean into uncomfortable conversations with humility, we're not just being "nice Christians"—we're doing **spiritual warfare**. Every time you lay down your pride and pick up grace, every time you refuse to gossip, every time you extend forgiveness instead of cutting someone off—you are **reclaiming territory** for the Kingdom of God.

I've seen this in my own life. Some of the most anointed seasons of ministry came right after I had hard conversations that led to reconciliation. And some of the driest seasons came when I ignored tension or let offense linger. The enemy wants you isolated, offended, and bitter. God wants you connected, healed, and free.

So if you're serious about seeking first the Kingdom, you have to get serious about fighting for your relationships. Not passively hoping they work out—but praying for them, prioritizing them, and protecting them like your purpose depends on it… because it does.

The Kingdom Perspective on Relationships

Life is all about love. God is love, and everything He created revolves around it. As believers, the most important lesson we are called to learn is how to love—unconditionally and sacrificially. Relationships, whether with family, friends, colleagues, or strangers, are the training ground where we cultivate this divine calling.

Jesus, in His life on earth, set the perfect example. He poured into His disciples, dined with sinners, forgave those who wronged Him, and ultimately laid down His life for us. His relationships were defined by humility, intentionality, and a willingness to serve. He demonstrated that real greatness in the Kingdom comes not from status or power, but from love and service.

In John 13:34, Jesus gives us a new commandment: "Love one another. As I have loved you, so you must love one another." This is the foundation of how we are to approach every relationship.

Practical Steps to Seek First in Your Relationships

Forgive Quickly

Forgiveness is not just a choice; it's a command in God's Kingdom. Ephesians 4:32 tells us, "Be kind and compassionate to one another, forgiving each other, just as in Christ God forgave you." When we hold on to bitterness or grudges, we rob ourselves of peace and hinder our relationship with God. Let go quickly, just as God has forgiven you.

Speak Life with Your Words

Words have the power to build or destroy. Proverbs 18:21 reminds us, "The tongue has the power of life and death." Be intentional with your words—use them to encourage, uplift, and bring healing to those around you. Every conversation is an opportunity to reflect God's love.

Invest in Meaningful Connections

Relationships thrive when they are nurtured. Whether it's spending quality time with family, offering a listening ear to a friend, or reaching out to a stranger, invest in those around you. Show love through intentional actions, not just words.

Prioritize Quality Time

Deuteronomy 6:6-7 stresses the importance of teaching and sharing God's Word within our families. Make space for regular family devotionals, date nights, or one-on-one moments with your spouse or children. In a busy world, these moments of intentional connection are priceless.

Practice Acts of Kindness

Acts of kindness are a simple yet profound way to live out the Gospel. Luke 6:35 calls us to love our enemies, do good to them, and lend without expecting anything in return. Choose to show kindness, especially to those who can't repay you—it reflects the heart of Jesus. Love isn't just a feeling; it's a choice to act, even when it's hard.

Resolve Conflicts Quickly

Conflict is inevitable, but the damage comes when it's left unresolved. Ephesians 4:26-27 warns against allowing anger to fester, saying, "Do not let the sun go down while you are still angry." Actively seek reconciliation before resentment can take root. Reconciliation isn't optional in the Kingdom—it's the heart of the Gospel.

Biblical Example: Jesus and His Disciples

Jesus exemplified all of these principles in His relationship with His disciples. He served them by washing their feet, teaching them, and investing in their growth. Even when they made mistakes, Jesus responded with patience, correction, and love. He showed that the heart of Kingdom relationships is rooted in humility, sacrifice, and intentionality.

In John 13:12-17, when Jesus washed His disciples' feet, He demonstrated that true greatness in God's Kingdom comes from serving others. He lived out the truth that relationships are meant to be marked by love, sacrifice, and mutual care.

Speak Life: Daily Declarations

"The tongue has the power of life and death, and those who love it will eat its fruit." — Proverbs 18:21

Relationships are spiritual ground. The way you speak about others—and to others—shapes your connection, your healing, and your legacy. Declare these truths daily over your relationships, your marriage, your friendships, and your future connections. Let your words be the foundation of a love that reflects the Kingdom.

7 Declarations to Strengthen Kingdom Relationships

- I choose to love others as Christ loves me—unconditionally, sacrificially, and faithfully.
- My words bring life, healing, and encouragement to everyone I encounter.
- I forgive quickly and pursue reconciliation, knowing

relationships are worth fighting for.

- I invest in meaningful, Christ-centered connections that reflect Heaven's values.
- My relationships are built on humility, grace, and mutual service—not pride or performance.
- I guard against offense, gossip, and division—choosing unity even when it's hard.

  I am a carrier of Kingdom love, and my relationships are a testimony of God's grace.

Speak these daily and watch how God begins to heal, strengthen, and multiply the impact of your relationships.

Prayer

Lord, thank You for the people You've placed in my life. Relationships are a gift—and I don't want to take them lightly. Help me love others the way You've loved me: with grace, humility, patience, and strength. Forgive me for any pride, offense, or selfishness that's gotten in the way. Give me the courage to pursue peace, the humility to say "I'm sorry," and the strength to forgive quickly and fully. Teach me to speak life, to listen well, and to build connection over convenience. Let every relationship in my life reflect Your love and carry Your presence. Use my words, my time, and my heart to point people to You. May my life be filled with relationships that honor You and bring You glory. In Jesus' name, Amen.

Call to Action: Fight for Connection

The enemy wants your relationships to fracture. But God wants them to flourish. Don't wait passively for your relationships to grow stronger—fight for them with intentionality, humility, and love. Let this be the week you realign your connections with God's Kingdom.

Step 1: Forgive & Reconcile

Think of someone you've been holding bitterness toward—or someone you need to forgive. Take the first step. Whether it's a message, a phone call, or simply a prayer—release the offense and invite God to restore.

Challenge: Write down their name and pray for them daily for the next 7 days. Ask God to soften your heart and open a door for reconciliation.

Step 2: Speak Life Daily

Be intentional with your words this week. Speak encouragement, truth, and kindness—especially in moments of stress or conflict.

Challenge: Text or speak one life-giving word to a different person each day. Bonus: Encourage someone who can't repay you.

Step 3: Make Time for Connection

Relationships don't grow without investment. This week, plan one meaningful moment with someone—a devotional with your spouse, coffee with a friend, a call with a relative, or lunch with someone new.

Challenge: Ask intentional questions that go deeper than surface-level. Let your presence carry peace.

Step 4: Invite Someone into Your Faith Journey

Ask God to highlight someone who's ready for more—and invite them into your walk. It could be starting a weekly prayer call, reading Scripture together, or simply offering to disciple them one step at a time. Don't wait for "official ministry"—your relationships *are* the ministry.

Step 5: Share Your Story

If God speaks to you, restores a relationship, or shows you something through this challenge—share it. Use the hashtag #SeekFirstChallenge to testify and invite others to restore and rebuild relationships in Jesus' name.

Seeking first in your relationships means leading with love, letting go of offense, and choosing connection over comfort. When you do, you're not just building better relationships—you're advancing God's Kingdom one heart at a time.

Relationships are Kingdom ground.

When we walk in love, unity, and humility, Heaven shows up. The people around you aren't just part of your life—they're part of your assignment.

Love them well. Forgive quickly. Stay available. That's where revival starts.

At the center of the Kingdom is love—and your relationships are where it's meant to be lived out.

Seeking first in your relationships means choosing connection over convenience, forgiveness over offense, and mission over pride.

"Love isn't just what we feel—it's how we reflect Heaven."
"Unity doesn't come from being the same. It comes from being surrendered to the same King."
"People may forget what you said, but they'll remember how you made them feel—and Who they saw in you."

So be intentional. Be present. Be loving.

Whether it's your marriage, your friendships, your family, or even that person who's hard to love—God is calling you to reflect His heart.

Want more ways to strengthen your Kingdom relationships?
Scan the QR code:

SEEK FIRST: RELATIONSHIPS

Love is the language of the Kingdom.
Speak it fluently. Live it **boldly.**

Chapter 9: Seek First Kingdom Building Pillar #7

The ultimate call on every believer's life is to partner with God in building His Kingdom. It's not about building our name—it's about advancing His mission.

Key Verse: *"Go therefore and make disciples of all nations..." (Matthew 28:19)*

Kingdom building isn't just for pastors or missionaries. It's for every believer. If you're a business owner, an artist, a teacher, a parent—you are called to build. The question is: are you building for Heaven or for yourself?

A Life on Mission

I grew up in the church. I remember hearing powerful testimonies and watching amazing preachers and bold evangelists online, especially on YouTube. I was in awe of how God used them, but deep down, I felt unqualified to ever be used like that. I hadn't gone to seminary, and I didn't naturally have a bold personality. So I believed the lie that I didn't have what it took to do anything great for the Kingdom.

But that was exactly what it was—a lie from the enemy.

The truth is, God doesn't call the qualified; He qualifies the called. And He has called you! In fact, God often chooses unlikely vessels—people the world would never expect—so that HE gets all the glory and no one can boast.

When you read the amazing stories in the book of Acts, don't just read them as history—read them as invitation. God still moves today, and He wants to move through you. Your calling may look different from mine or someone else's, but every believer has a role to play. Whatever gift, passion, or platform God has entrusted to you, He wants to use it to build His Kingdom.

There is no greater purpose than this. God didn't create us to be spectators. He invites us to be participants in His redemptive work in the world. So get excited—He is moving in these days, and you are a part of it. Let's advance His Kingdom together!

We live in a world that desperately needs Jesus. And the greatest way we can honor Him is by living on mission. That doesn't mean you have to move to another country. It means living every day with the awareness that God wants to use you, right where you are.

But here's something that will shift everything if you let it:

With God, Not Just For God

There's a big difference between building *for* God and building *with* God. Many well-meaning believers spend their lives trying to do great things *for* God—launching ministries, starting businesses, leading people—but burn out or lose clarity because they're doing it in their own strength.

But God never asked us to build alone. He's not looking for more performers. He's looking for *partners*. He doesn't just want your effort—He wants your obedience, your dependence, and your friendship. He wants to walk with you, guide you, and co-labor with you in everything you do.

This changed everything for me.

There was a time I was doing things that looked great on the outside—outreach, ministry, projects—but I hadn't asked God if He even called me to that specific thing. I was carrying weight He never asked me to carry. I was building for Him, but not with Him.

When I stopped striving and started surrendering, my mindset shifted from performance to presence. I learned that obedience is better than opportunity. And fruitfulness doesn't come from hustle—it comes from abiding (John 15:5).

When you build with God, you don't just work *for* the Kingdom—you release Heaven on Earth. You become a vessel through which God does more than you ever could on your own. That's when Kingdom building becomes supernatural.

Building the Kingdom means saying "yes" to God's promptings. It means sharing the Gospel boldly, discipling others intentionally, and using your time, talent, and treasure to expand Heaven's influence on Earth.

Practical Ways to Build God's Kingdom

Share the Gospel Often

Ask God for boldness. Look for opportunities. Your story can change lives.

Make Disciples

It's not about perfection—it's about intentionality. Walk with people. Teach them what you know. Multiply your faith.

Your Gifts for Impact

Every skill you have can serve the Kingdom. Use your creativity, business, leadership, or compassion to reflect God.

Live with Generosity

Your resources are not just for you. Invest in missions, ministries, and people who are advancing the Gospel.

Obey the Holy Spirit Quickly

When He nudges you, go. Prompt obedience releases power and reveals God to the world.

Speak Life: Daily Declarations

"The tongue has the power of life and death, and those who love it will eat its fruit." — Proverbs 18:21

Your words release authority. When you declare God's mission over your life, something activates in the spirit realm. Speak these truths boldly, and watch how your heart aligns, your boldness increases, and Heaven flows through you.

7 Declarations for Kingdom Builders

- I am a Kingdom builder, and my life is on mission every day.
- I boldly share the Gospel, knowing my story carries power

and purpose.

- I disciple others intentionally—I don't keep the truth to myself.
- I use my gifts, passions, and resources to expand God's Kingdom, not my own.
  I hear the voice of the Holy Spirit and obey without delay.
- I am not a spectator—I'm a participant in Heaven's movement on Earth.
- My life is a vessel for revival, impact, and eternal legacy.

Speak these every morning and let them drive your purpose, passion, and boldness.

Prayer

Jesus, thank You for the honor of being called into Your mission. I say yes again today—not to religion or performance, but to walking with You in power and purpose. Use my life to bring the Gospel to every space You send me. I don't want to build apart from You—I want to build *with* You. Show me where to go, who to reach, and what to release. Give me boldness to share truth, humility to disciple others, and clarity to invest my time and talents where they matter most. Let everything I build be grounded in obedience and fueled by love. May I never settle for comfort over calling. Make my life count for eternity. In Your mighty name, Amen.

Call to Action: Build What Matters Most

You weren't saved to sit—you were saved to build. Kingdom building isn't just for pastors or missionaries—it's for every believer who says yes to Jesus. When you step into your calling, you step into the mission of Heaven.

Here's how to start building what truly lasts:

Step 1: Identify Your Kingdom Assignment

Ask the Holy Spirit: *"What part of Your Kingdom have You assigned to me right now?"*
Is it your family? Your workplace? A creative idea? A neighbor? Write down what comes to mind—then pray over it this week and ask, *"What's my next step of obedience?"*

Step 2: Start Where You Are

Don't wait for the perfect conditions to get started. Share your testimony with someone. Start the small group. Offer to pray with a coworker. Launch the podcast. Open your home. Obedience always precedes clarity.

Step 3: Support a Kingdom Builder

Look around. Who's already building something for God's glory? Find a way to encourage, serve, sow into, or promote what they're doing. When you build with others, you multiply impact and protect your own heart from isolation or comparison.

Step 4: Create Your Kingdom Builder's Creed

Write your own declaration of purpose. Something like:
"I am a Kingdom builder. I will use my time, my voice, my gifts, and my

resources to advance the Gospel, love people well, and finish strong." Print it. Post it. Say it out loud this week.

You have something the Kingdom needs.
God doesn't need your résumé—He wants your yes. And He's not looking for perfection. He's looking for people who will show up with surrendered hearts and willing hands.

It's time to build—one obedient step at a time.

Kingdom Over Comfort

You were not saved to sit—you were saved to build.
Kingdom building isn't reserved for the stage. It happens in the classroom, on the job site, at the dinner table, and in the streets. It's not about your title—it's about your yes.

"God isn't looking for the most qualified—He's looking for the most surrendered."
"The Great Commission wasn't a suggestion—it's our mission."
"The Kingdom moves at the speed of your obedience."
"Don't just read Acts—live it."

You were born for such a time as this. The world needs what God placed inside you.
So step out, speak up, and build with boldness. Every conversation, every act of love, every seed sown in obedience—it all counts for eternity.

Want to keep growing as a Kingdom builder? Scan the QR code:

SEEK FIRST: KINGDOM BUILDING

Let's not just be believers. Let's be builders.

Chapter 10: Seek First: A Call to Action

God has called you to participate in His Kingdom work (Ephesians 2:10). The Christian life isn't a passive existence—it's the greatest adventure filled with purpose, power, and eternal impact. You were created for such a time as this, uniquely positioned by God to fulfill a role in His divine plan. The question is: will you step into it boldly?

When Obedience Was the Only Qualification

In those early days of stepping out in faith, I wasn't just battling thoughts of inadequacy—I was also wrestling with something deeper: the fear of man. I would often ask God how to overcome it. I wanted to boldly share the Gospel, but every time I thought about approaching someone, I felt that familiar tension—What will they think of me? Will I look crazy? Will I sound weird? I didn't realize it at the time, but all that fear was rooted in pride. When the Lord revealed that to me, I was surprised. Pride? Really? But as I examined it more closely, I saw the truth. My fear of rejection was because I was still focused on myself—how I would be perceived, how I would look, what they might think of me. It was self-preservation disguised as humility. The focus was on me, and that's what was causing the fear.

But things began to shift when I started praying a simple but powerful prayer: "God, help me see people the way You see them." That prayer began to change everything. As I looked at people through the eyes of the Father, my heart softened. I began to feel deep compassion and love for those I once hesitated to approach. I wasn't thinking about myself anymore—I was burdened with the reality of how much God loves that person in front of me. And in that place of love, fear lost its grip. Scripture says, "Perfect love casts out all fear" (1 John 4:18), and I can testify to that truth. Once I stopped thinking about how people would see me and started caring more about how God sees them, the fear faded and boldness rose up.

That's what led to the birth of our ministry, Love on Hamilton. It didn't begin with a polished plan or a big platform—it started with a simple yes. A commitment to go to the streets every week, rain or shine, with or without a crowd. We prayed. We shared. We loved. And we watched God move in powerful ways. People were healed, lives were transformed, souls were saved—not because we were impressive, but because we were available.

So if you're struggling with fear, if you're unsure of what to say or worried about what people will think, I hope this encourages you. The truth is, God wants to use you in powerful ways. Don't wait for a title, a mic, or a moment where everything feels perfect. Just take the first step. Fix your eyes on Jesus. See people through His love. And remember: your availability is more important than your ability. He doesn't need your résumé—He just wants your yes.

The Call You Were Made For

Seeking first the Kingdom isn't just about personal devotion—it's about action. It's about carrying the Gospel into the world, walking in the authority Jesus gave you, and serving with a heart that reflects His love.

- **Share the Gospel (Matthew 28:19):** Your story has power. It carries the evidence of God's goodness, the reality of His grace, and the hope that can transform lives.

- **Walk in the Authority of Christ (Luke 10:19):** You've been given power over darkness. The enemy trembles when a believer knows their authority and walks in it.
- **Serve Others with Humility (Philippians 2:3-4):** True greatness in the Kingdom is found in servanthood. When you put others before yourself, you reflect the heart of Jesus.

A Kingdom-focused life isn't lived on the sidelines—it's lived on the frontlines of faith, where God moves through you to impact the world.

The Effect of One Step of Faith

Imagine a young man named Jason. He works a regular job, attends church, and prays occasionally, but deep down, he feels like he's just going through the motions. One day, he decides to step out in faith. Instead of walking past a struggling coworker, he stops and prays for them. That simple act of obedience leads to a conversation where he shares the Gospel. The coworker surrenders their life to Christ. Jason realizes something powerful: faith isn't just about knowing—it's about doing. He starts praying for opportunities every day. Soon, he's leading Bible studies, discipling new believers, and seeing lives change. What started with one act of obedience became a Kingdom movement. Every great move of God starts with a single step of faith. What step is God calling you to take? - I like to say: **'Never doubt what God can do with a small seed sown'**

Challenge: Step Into Bold Faith

Faith isn't meant to stay in the realm of ideas—it's meant to be lived out. Here's how you can start:

- **Share Your Testimony:** Someone needs to hear how God has transformed your life.
- **Pray for Someone:** Prayer is powerful. It invites Heaven into earthly situations.
- **Start a Ministry or Outreach:** You don't need a big platform—just a willing heart.
- **Ask Yourself Daily:** *How did I seek God first today?*

Fueling the Fire Within You

John Piper challenges believers in *Don't Waste Your Life*: *"You don't have to know a lot of things for your life to make a lasting difference in the world. But you do need to know the few great, unchanging, obvious, simple, glorious things—and be set on fire by them."*

That fire comes from knowing Christ and living fully surrendered to His mission.

Practical Steps to Kingdom Impact

- **Daily Evangelism Goal:** Commit to sharing the Gospel or praying for someone every day (Matthew 28:19).
- **Live with Eternal Perspective:** Evaluate how your daily actions impact eternity (2 Corinthians 4:18).
- **Join a Kingdom Movement:** Get involved in missions, outreach, or prayer groups (Isaiah 6:8).

The Disciples' Bold Obedience

The early disciples were ordinary men who became extraordinary world-changers simply because they obeyed Jesus. They stepped out in faith, relied on the Holy Spirit, and turned the world upside down (Acts 1:8). If God could use fishermen, tax collectors, and outcasts to launch the greatest movement in history, He can use you too.

Speak Life: Daily Declarations

"The tongue has the power of life and death, and those who love it will eat its fruit." — Proverbs 18:21

Your obedience has the power to shift lives—and it starts with the words you declare. When you speak faith, courage, and surrender over your life, boldness rises and fear breaks. You weren't saved to sit—you were saved to be sent. Declare these truths daily and step into the adventure.

7 Declarations for a Life of Bold Obedience

- I am called and equipped by God to make an eternal impact.
- I walk in the authority of Christ, and I will not be held back by fear.
- I choose faith over comfort and boldness over passivity.
- My life is an adventure—partnering with the Holy Spirit in every step.
- I carry the power of the Gospel and the compassion of Jesus.
- I go where He sends me, speak when He prompts me, and trust Him with the outcome.
- I seek first the Kingdom of God and trust Him to provide, lead, and multiply my yes.

  Speak these every morning as a battle cry—and then move like they're true.

Prayer

Lord, thank You for the call You've placed on my life. I know You didn't save me to play it safe—I was made to move mountains, to reach people, and to live boldly for Your glory.Today, I surrender my fears, my comfort, and my excuses. Fill me with the power of the Holy Spirit. Let boldness rise in me like never before. I don't want to just believe in the Gospel—I want to carry it. I want to live it. I want to give it away freely, just as I've received. Lead me to the people who need hope. Speak through me. Move through me. Use me in ways I've never imagined. I say yes to the mission, and I say yes to You. In Jesus' name, Amen.

Call to Action: Step Into the Mission

You weren't called to be a bystander in the Kingdom—you were born to be a warrior. This chapter is more than a conclusion—it's a commissioning. Don't let the momentum stop here. You weren't created to coast—you were created to carry the Kingdom. Every truth you've read in this book was meant to lead you to this moment: bold, daily obedience. The kind that shifts atmospheres, shakes fear, and impacts eternity.

Now it's time to activate everything you've learned:

Step 1: Commit to Living Sent

You don't need a stage, a title, or a spotlight. You just need your feet and a surrendered heart. Write this somewhere you'll see it often: "Wherever my feet go, the Kingdom goes with me."Say it every morning. Let it be your daily reminder that you are on assignment—at home, at work, at the gym, in the grocery store.

Step 2: Share the Gospel Boldly This Week

Ask God for one opportunity this week to share the Gospel with someone. It might be a full conversation, a prayer, a testimony, or even a simple act of love that opens the door. Don't overthink it. Just look up and obey.

Step 3: Start Your Gospel Rhythm

Pick one day a week to dedicate to intentional outreach. Pray, walk your neighborhood, go to the streets, or reach out online. Call it your "Kingdom Day." Write it into your calendar. No excuses.

Step 4: Launch What's on Your Heart

What has God been nudging you to start? A podcast? A business? A prayer group? A YouTube channel? A mentoring group? Don't let fear delay your assignment. Break the inertia. Make one move this week. Text someone. Buy the domain. Design the logo. Write the intro. Start.

Step 5: Create Your Personal "Seek First Manifesto"

Write 5-10 declarations that define how you will live going forward. Example:

- I will seek God before anything else.
- I will live to please Heaven, not impress people.
- I will speak life, give generously, and obey quickly.
- I will build what matters.

Read this every week. Let it recalibrate you when life gets loud.

God didn't call you to safety—He called you to surrender. He didn't save you to sit—He saved you to go. Your life, your voice, your obedience—it matters.

The world doesn't need more comfortable Christians. It needs Seek First Warriors.

Men and women who live surrendered, speak boldly, love radically, and carry Heaven wherever they go. And that's you.

Now go—**live the Seek First life**… and never look back.

This is your moment. Take the step. Live the mission.
Welcome to the front lines.

Conclusion: Living the Seek First Life

This Book Was a Step of Faith

"But seek first His Kingdom and His righteousness, and all these things will be given to you as well." — Matthew 6:33

If I'm being honest with you—writing this book wasn't something I ever saw myself doing. I don't consider myself a writer. I've spent most of my life swinging hammers, managing job sites, and working with my hands—not sitting behind a desk typing out sentences. This whole process felt like a stretch. I had all the doubts you'd expect: *"Who am I to write a book? What if no one reads it? When will I even find the time?"* I wrestled with that inner voice that tries to disqualify you before you even begin.

But here's what I've learned—when God puts something on your heart, your job isn't to have it all figured out. It's not to analyze it to death or wait until it feels convenient or comfortable. Your job is simply to obey. To say yes.

This book is my yes.

It's not perfect. It's not polished like a professional writer's work. But it's real. And it's obedient. It came from a place of deep conviction—because I believe this message matters. Not because it's from me, but because it's *from Him.* I wrote this book as a tool to serve you, to encourage you, to challenge you, and to remind you that your story matters too. That the same God who called me out of my comfort zone is calling you into something greater as well.

Maybe while reading this, something inside you began to stir. A dream. A vision. A message you've been carrying for years. Maybe God's been whispering something to your heart—an idea, a shift, a step of obedience that's felt just a little too risky. If that's you, let me encourage you: **don't wait until you feel qualified.**

Just take the first step.

Because the truth is, if God called you to it, He's already made a way through it. If He placed the burden on your heart, He'll provide the grace to walk it out. He doesn't ask for perfection—He asks for obedience. And obedience always opens doors you could never open on your own.

You don't need to be the best, the smartest, or the most experienced. You just need to be *available*. The world needs what God placed inside of you just as much as what He placed inside of me. So go write that book. Start that business. Launch that ministry. Lead the group. Share the Gospel. Pray for that stranger. Tell your story.

And if you're scared? Do it scared. But do it.

Because you have no idea what God will do with one simple act of obedience. I'm living proof of that. And I believe with everything in me—you will be too.

The decision to seek God first isn't just a one-time commitment—it's a lifestyle. A posture of the heart. A daily surrender. And honestly? It's the greatest adventure of your life. It means putting His presence above your plans, trusting His process over your preferences, and allowing Him to shape your desires instead of chasing your own ambitions. It means letting go of temporary success and choosing eternal significance. It's not about chasing blessings—it's about chasing the One who *is* the blessing.

And when you really start to live like that—when you seek first His Kingdom in everything—you begin to see life differently. You live with purpose. You walk with confidence. You rest in peace. Because you're no longer building on shifting sand—you're building on the solid foundation of Jesus.

Paul said it best: *"I consider everything a loss because of the surpassing worth of knowing Christ Jesus my Lord"* (Philippians 3:8). That's what this whole Seek First life is about—valuing Jesus above all else, and letting every part of your life flow from that place of devotion.

Your highest calling isn't to build a platform. It's not to impress people or chase influence.

Your greatest calling is to build the Kingdom.

The Ripple Effect of Obedience

Your obedience isn't just for you—it's for generations.

When you seek first the Kingdom, your life becomes a seed. Your "yes" could lead to someone else's salvation. Your boldness might break the fear off someone watching from afar. Your willingness to be used by God may unlock someone else's purpose.

This is how revival begins. Not just in church buildings—but in homes, workplaces, coffee shops, gyms, schools, and grocery stores. Everywhere your feet go becomes Kingdom territory when you carry His presence and live surrendered to His will.

Never underestimate what God can do through a fully surrendered life. History shows us that some of the greatest movements of God started with ordinary people who simply said, "Yes."

When you step into your calling, you're not just obeying for today—you're creating ripple effects that will echo into eternity.

You may never see the full impact of your obedience on this side of Heaven, but one day, you'll stand before God and see the harvest of every seed you sowed.

So don't shrink back.
Don't disqualify yourself.
And don't wait until it makes sense.
If He's calling, say yes.

And What Happens When You Do That?

When you truly say yes to building the Kingdom—not just in theory, but with your whole life—you become part of something bigger than yourself. Something eternal. You shift from survival mode to assignment mode. You stop striving to build your own name and start pouring yourself out for His glory.

You start to see that the things of this world were never meant to satisfy you. That God's presence is your true reward. That legacy isn't about what people say about you—it's about the impact your obedience has for generations to come.

You start showing up differently—in your home, at your job, in your city. You stop waiting for revival to come from a stage or a preacher and start realizing *you* carry revival, because Christ lives in you. Your yes becomes a seed. Your obedience becomes a spark. And before you know it, your life becomes the very thing someone else needed to encounter God.

That's the power of a Seek First life.

It's not always flashy. It won't always make sense to the world. But it's the only life worth living. One built on the Word. Fueled by the Spirit. Rooted in Jesus. And pointed toward eternity.

So I leave you with this:

Seek Him when it's quiet. Seek Him when it's loud.
Seek Him when you're winning. Seek Him when you're weary.
Seek Him when you don't know what's next.
Seek Him when everything is falling into place—and when everything feels like it's falling apart.
Seek Him first. Always.
Because when you do, everything else—your purpose, your provision, your peace—will follow.

I'm cheering you on. I'm praying for you. And I'm believing that your best days are ahead.

Now go live the Seek First life!
—Daniel Ziedins

Live the Seek First Life

Start Your Day with Surrender

- Before checking your phone or planning your schedule, acknowledge God as first in your life. Pray, "Lord, I seek

You first today. Lead me in Your ways."

- Meditate on Matthew 6:33 each morning as a foundation for your day.

Put Faith into Action

- Share your testimony with someone this week. Your story has the power to change lives (Revelation 12:11).
- Look for ways to serve others daily, whether through an encouraging word, a selfless act, or intentional kindness (Galatians 5:13).

Keep an Eternal Perspective

- Regularly evaluate your goals and decisions. Are they driven by Kingdom priorities or earthly distractions? (Colossians 3:2)
- Invest your time in things that last—prayer, outreach, discipleship, and building relationships that point people to Jesus (2 Timothy 2:2).

Stay Connected to the Body of Christ

- Surround yourself with believers who push you closer to God (Hebrews 10:24-25).
- Seek mentorship and accountability to keep you on track in your faith journey.

Celebrate the Journey

- Keep a record of answered prayers, testimonies, and moments when God shows up. Reflect on His faithfulness and let it fuel your trust in Him.

You've been equipped, challenged, and called—now go walk it out. Live boldly. Love deeply. Build the Kingdom.

Speak Life: Daily Declarations

"The tongue has the power of life and death, and those who love it will eat its fruit." — Proverbs 18:21

You've been equipped, called, and commissioned. Now speak like it. The way you talk about your life, your purpose, and your calling shapes the atmosphere around you. Let these declarations anchor you in a life of purpose and power.

7 Declarations to Live the Seek First Life

1. I seek first the Kingdom of God and trust Him to provide all I need.
2. My life is rooted in eternal purpose—not temporary success or worldly gain.
3. I am a vessel of God's power, love, and truth to everyone I encounter.
4. I boldly walk in the dreams and assignments God has placed in my heart.
5. I obey immediately, knowing God uses every step to shape my destiny.
6. I live in joyful surrender, trusting that His plans are greater than my own.
7. I am part of something bigger—my life is a Kingdom legacy in motion.

Speak these aloud every day—and let your life follow your words.

Prayer

Heavenly Father, thank You for calling me into a life of purpose, joy, and eternal impact. I don't want to just believe in You—I want to live fully surrendered to You. Teach me to seek first Your Kingdom and Your righteousness, not just once, but daily. Align my desires with Yours. Help me trust You completely, obey You boldly, and follow You wholeheartedly. Fill me with Your Spirit so that I may carry light, love, and truth everywhere I go. Use my life as a vessel of Your glory. May everything I do reflect the surpassing worth of knowing Christ Jesus my Lord. This is my "yes." Now lead me where You want me to go. In Jesus' name, Amen.

Call to Action: Live the Movement

This isn't the end of a book—it's the beginning of a lifestyle. You've been equipped to live differently, think eternally, and walk boldly. Now, it's time to activate it.

Step 1: Become a Seek First Ambassador

Commit to fully living the Seek First life. Don't just talk about it—walk it. Embody Matthew 6:33 in your decisions, your relationships, your business, your time, and your dreams.
Challenge: Write out your personal Seek First mission statement and share it with someone close to you—or post it with the hashtag #SeekFirstChallenge.

Step 2: Inspire the Circle Around You

Your story matters. Start sharing it. Tell people what God is doing in your life and encourage them to join the movement.

Challenge: Host a Seek First conversation with a friend or small group this month. Invite others into the journey.

Step 3: Stay Anchored in the Word

Every lasting life change starts with time in God's presence. Make prayer, Scripture, and worship non-negotiables.
Challenge: Choose one Seek First verse from this book to meditate on every morning for the next 7 days. Journal what God speaks to you.

Step 4: Step Into the Dream

Don't shelf the vision God gave you. Don't delay the obedience. Take one bold step toward the thing God placed in your heart.
Challenge: Write it down, make a move, and invite someone to hold you accountable. Action activates anointing.

You were made for this.

Final Charge: You Are a Seek First Warrior

Congratulations on completing this book!
I consider you a Seek First Warrior—someone who's not just a hearer of the Word, but a doer. You've taken a powerful step toward living a life of eternal impact. I truly believe incredible things are ahead for you. You are now a threat to the kingdom of darkness, and by God's grace, you will impact more lives and advance His Kingdom like never before. You were born for such a time as this. Keep shining. Keep building. The world needs the fire God has placed inside you.

Never forget:

You are a Warrior. God is with you. So Seek First.
I'll see you on the battlefield, Warrior!

Now I've got one big ask—share this message.
Take a picture of this book and post it on social media. Tag @SeekFirstBrand and include a quote or a testimony of how it impacted you. Your story could inspire someone else to start their own journey of putting God first.

We believe this isn't just a book—it's a movement.
A movement of people living boldly, loving radically, and seeking the Kingdom above all else.
You are part of that.

Also, leaving a short review online really helps us spread the word—it might seem small, but it makes a big difference!

And one last thing—come back to this book.

Pick it up again in a few months. Reread it. Revisit the challenges. Rework the declarations.
Each time you go through it, God will reveal something new that could change your life in ways you never imagined.

You're not done—this is just the beginning.

Keep seeking.
Keep building.
Keep living the Seek First life.

Stay Connected

Stay connected with our community at
SeekFirstBrand.com

Explore our Kingdom network at
ThyKingdom.Network

Connect with me, the author at
DanielZiedins.com

If you're new to this journey of faith, I want you to know: you're not alone. This next section is just for you:

NEW BELIEVER'S GUIDE TO THE SEEK FIRST LIFE

Whether you've recently given your life to Jesus, or you're still exploring what it means to follow Him, I want you to know something: you're not alone. You're part of a family now—a global family of believers who are learning to walk by faith, one step at a time.

If you're new to faith in Jesus—welcome to the family! This book may have introduced some spiritual concepts you've never heard before. Here's a quick guide to help you walk forward in clarity and confidence:

What is the Gospel?

The Gospel means "Good News." The Good News is this: Jesus Christ, the Son of God, came to earth, lived a sinless life, died on the cross for your sins, and rose again on the third day, conquering sin and death.

When you repent (turn away from your sin) and put your faith in Jesus as Savior and Lord, you are forgiven, made new, and brought into a restored relationship with God.

Scriptures:

"For God so loved the world that He gave His one and only Son, that whoever believes in Him shall not perish but have eternal life."

– John 3:16
"Repent, then, and turn to God, so that your sins may be wiped out..." – Acts 3:19

What is Salvation?

Salvation is a free gift from God. You don't earn it—it's received by repentance and faith in Jesus Christ. When you confess Him as Lord and believe He rose from the dead, you are saved and born again.

Scriptures:
"If you declare with your mouth, 'Jesus is Lord,' and believe in your heart that God raised Him from the dead, you will be saved." – Romans 10:9
"Godly sorrow brings repentance that leads to salvation and leaves no regret..." – 2 Corinthians 7:10

What is Baptism?

Baptism is an outward declaration of your inward transformation. It symbolizes dying to your old life and rising with Christ. Speak to a local church or mentor about getting baptized soon!

Scriptures:
"We were therefore buried with Him through baptism into death in order that... we too may live a new life." – Romans 6:4
"Repent and be baptized, every one of you, in the name of Jesus Christ for the forgiveness of your sins." – Acts 2:38

What is Fasting?

Fasting is when you voluntarily give something up—often food—for a set time to focus on God. It sharpens your spirit, clears distractions, and deepens your dependence on Him.

Scriptures:
"When you fast, do not look somber... But when you fast, anoint your head and wash your face." – Matthew 6:16–17
"Is not this the kind of fasting I have chosen: to loose the chains of injustice..." – Isaiah 58:6

What is Tithing?

Tithing is giving the first 10% of your income to God through your local church. It's an act of worship that demonstrates trust and honors God as your provider.

Scriptures:
"Bring the whole tithe into the storehouse... Test Me in this," says the Lord Almighty. – Malachi 3:10
"Each of you should give what you have decided in your heart to give... for God loves a cheerful giver." – 2 Corinthians 9:7

What is the Holy Spirit?

The Holy Spirit is God's presence living inside every believer. He is your helper, comforter, and guide. He empowers you to live a godly life, understand Scripture, and boldly walk in truth.

Scriptures:
"But you will receive power when the Holy Spirit comes on you; and you will be My witnesses..." – Acts 1:8
"The Advocate, the Holy Spirit... will teach you all things and will remind you of everything I have said to you." – John 14:26

Next Steps for You:

- Get plugged into a Bible-believing church
- Get a physical Bible and read daily (Start with the book of

John)

- Pray daily — prayer is simply talking to God
- Tell someone about your faith
- Ask God to show you your purpose

You're not alone.
Visit SeekFirstBrand.com & LoveonTheWorld.com to connect with others and grow in your new walk with Jesus.

Know someone just starting their journey with Jesus?

Don't keep this to yourself—give it away.

Buy a copy of Seek First for a friend, a new believer, or someone hungry for truth. Use it as a bold tool for evangelism. This isn't just a book—it's a spark.

Let's start a movement of everyday believers sharing the Gospel one book at a time.

Every soul matters. Every seed counts.

You carry the light—now pass it on!

SEEK FIRST

About the Author

Daniel Ziedins is a husband, father, and Kingdom builder dedicated to helping people live a life fully surrendered to Jesus. He is the founder of Love on The World and the Seek First Brand, inspiring believers worldwide to live with bold faith, eternal purpose, and daily discipline rooted in Matthew 6:33. Daniel's journey—from construction sites to entrepreneurship to street ministry—reflects a life transformed by obedience and anchored in truth. He lives in Ontario, Canada, with his wife Katie and daughter Ava, and currently serves in evangelism and network mobilizer with e3 Canada. You can connect with Daniel at DanielZiedins.com or follow along the various ministries at ThyKingdom.Network.

Remember...
You Are Loved!

Manufactured by Amazon.ca
Bolton, ON

45969587R00066